DISCOVERING U.S. HISTORY

The Civil War Era

1851–1865

DISCOVERING U.S. HISTORY

The New World: Prehistory–1542

Colonial America: 1543–1763

Revolutionary America: 1764–1789

Early National America: 1790–1850

The Civil War Era: 1851–1865

The New South and the Old West: 1866–1890

The Gilded Age and Progressivism: 1891–1913

World War I and the Roaring Twenties: 1914–1928

The Great Depression: 1929–1938

World War II: 1939–1945

The Cold War and Postwar America: 1946–1963

Modern America: 1964–Present

DISCOVERING U.S. HISTORY

The Civil War Era 1851–1865

Tim McNeese

Consulting Editor: Richard Jensen, Ph.D.

THE CIVIL WAR ERA: 1851–1865

Chelsea House
An imprint of Infobase Publishing
132 West 31st Street
New York NY 10001

Library of Congress Cataloging-in-Publication Data
McNeese, Tim.
The Civil War era, 1851–1865 / written by Tim McNeese.
p. cm. — (Discovering U.S. history ; v. 5)
Includes bibliographical references and index.
ISBN 978-1-60413-352-3 (hardcover : acid-free paper) 1. United States—History—Civil War, 1861–1865 —Juvenile literature. 2. United States—History—Civil War, 1861–1865—Causes—Juvenile literature. I. Title. II. Series

E468.M224 2009
973.7'11—dc22

2009003660

Chelsea House books are available at special discounts when purchased in bulk quantities for businesses, associations, institutions, or sales promotions. Please call our Special Sales Department in New York at (212) 967-8800 or (800) 322-8755.

You can find Chelsea House on the World Wide Web at http://www.chelseahouse.com

The Discovering U.S. History series was produced for Chelsea House by Bender Richardson White, Uxbridge, UK

Editors: Lionel Bender and Susan Malyan
Designer and Picture Researcher: Ben White
Production: Kim Richardson
Maps and graphics: Stefan Chabluk
Cover printed by Bang Printing, Brainerd, MN
Book printed and bound by Bang Printing, Brainerd, MN
Date printed: April 2010
Printed in the United States of America

10 9 8 7 6 5 4 3 2 1

This book is printed on acid-free paper.

Contents

Introduction
North Versus South

The air was crisp, and the sky clear, except for the pall of smoke to the northwest that hung like a shroud in the air. The date was November 16, 1864, and the sooty cloud signaled the ruin of the city of Atlanta, Georgia. Witnessing the scene that morning from a suburban hillside were those largely responsible for the city's destruction: 62,000 blue-clad soldiers of the Union Army, including 5,000 cavalrymen. They were Northerners who had been at war with the Confederate States of America for three-and-a-half years. A military band struck a favorite tune, "John Brown's Body," and many of the men joined in singing the chorus: "Glory, glory, hallelujah!" It was a beautiful day for a march.

THE MAN FROM OHIO

Overseeing this military drama was a tough-minded, no-nonsense Union general named William Tecumseh Sherman. He was born in 1820 and had attended West Point Military

Academy more than 20 years earlier. Sherman's first assignments had been postings in South Carolina and Florida, states that were now part of the Confederacy. He had been swept up in the gold rush of '49 and had resigned his officer's commission in 1853 to become a would-be banker in San Francisco. However, Sherman's business venture had not panned out, so his old military comrades, P.G.T. Beauregard and Braxton Bragg, now Confederate generals, had secured him an appointment as superintendent of the Louisiana State Seminary of Learning and Military Academy. Sherman had thrived during those years in the South and had come to love much that was southern. But those days were now gone. The South, for Major General William Tecumseh Sherman, had become the home of his enemy, and therefore a military target.

The war Sherman was now a part of had begun in April 1861, when his old friend Beauregard had ordered the bombardment of Fort Sumter, a federal military garrison post on an island in Charleston Harbor. For years previously Southerners had suggested and discussed the possibility of seceding from the Union, of dissolving their ties of brotherhood and patriot allegiance to the United States of America. Issues and controversies had swirled around slavery and its extension into the American West. Time and again the politicians had negotiated and come to terms, despite their disagreements. But the day had finally arrived when the South reached its emotional and political breaking point.

Disagreement Turns to War

The election of Abraham Lincoln to the presidency had served as the immediate catalyst for secession. When Lincoln, a Northerner and a Republican, was elected in November 1860 Southerners believed the country had chosen a leader who had no sympathy for the South. They believed he was an abolitionist, one who was opposed to slavery and supported its immediate destruction. Lincoln was no abolitionist in 1860, but that truth almost did not matter. The Illinois Republican had been elected without a single Southern vote. From Texas to Florida to Virginia, Southerners were certain that the future would consist of their voices being silenced and their "peculiar institution"—slavery—being doomed.

One by one, 11 Southern states had seceded from the Union and formed their own country. When Lincoln was unwilling to turn federal property on Southern soil over to the Confederates, they chose to attack, starting at Fort Sumter. Between April 1861 and November 1864 Americans on both sides had killed one another in a random collection of conflicts. In battle after battle—First Bull Run, Shiloh, the Seven Days, Second Bull Run, Antietam, Chancellorsville, Gettysburg—the clash of arms had delivered thousands, even tens of thousands of casualties. Yet Americans had continued to fight, each committed to their own cause and certain that God was on their side.

Atlanta Falls

When the war opened, William Tecumseh Sherman had reenlisted, as a colonel. He rose rapidly through the ranks, serving in the western theater of war, in Tennessee, Kentucky, and Mississippi. By the summer of 1864, already a brigadier general, Sherman had received orders to launch a campaign of conquest from Chattanooga, Tennessee, marching southeast toward Georgia's most important city—Atlanta. It was a hub city, an urban center for converging rail lines and communications. Atlanta represented a bastion of defiance, of Southern strength, even as the Confederate armies were losing battles, their manpower nearly exhausted, and their supplies nearly nonexistent.

In early May, Sherman and his men had begun the march toward Atlanta, repeatedly engaging an outnumbered Confederate force under the command of General Joseph Johnston.

Abraham Lincoln, 16th president of the United States, as photographed in 1864. He was opposed to slavery but was willing to allow it in the South in order to keep the states united.

The generals had known one another before the war. Twenty years later, in 1884, Joe Johnston would serve as a pall-bearer at Sherman's funeral. But for now, they were enemies. That was the nature of the American Civil War. Men who knew one another well were now fighting one another, a reality they had never dreamed of before the conflict began. West Point roommates met one another on opposite sides of the field of battle. Commanders ordered their artillery to fire on the enemy, knowing an old friend would be put in harm's way and may be killed.

With each clash of arms between Johnston and Sherman, the Union Army was gaining ground. The President of the Confederacy, Jefferson Davis, had, by mid-July, replaced Johnston, convinced he was not fighting hard enough. He selected a tough Texan, a no-nonsense 33-year-old commander named John Bell Hood. During the weeks that followed Hood threw everything he had at Sherman, despite being outnumbered dramatically. On July 20, just days after taking command, he struck at Sherman at Peachtree Creek outside Atlanta, then again two days later, after an overnight march that exhausted his men. But the Confederates could not hold back the tidal wave of Federal forces that were pressing them. By early September Atlanta was in Union hands.

OPENING THE WAY

Atlanta was not the state capital at that time, but it was a prize indeed for Sherman. The city had nearly doubled in population to 20,000 since the start of the war. The Confederacy had turned Atlanta into a steam-powered manufacturing town, with foundries, gun plants, munitions factories, and rail supply warehouses and depots scattered everywhere. Confederate President Jefferson Davis had long recognized the value of Atlanta to the Confederate states, asserting, as recorded by historian A. A. Hoehling, that its fall would:

> *Open the way for the Federal Army to the Gulf on the one hand, and to Charleston on the other, and close up those rich granaries from which Lee's armies are supplied. It would give them control of our network of railways and thus paralyze our efforts.*

Sherman's capture of Atlanta had only brought Davis's fears to reality. The city was lost; it would no longer contribute to the Confederate cause. But this loss was to prove only the beginning. While resting his men for a month, Sherman repeatedly noted the presence of Hood's army, which was still in the field. The Confederate troops were constantly harassing the Union general's only supply line, the Chattanooga-to-Atlanta railroad, which he had utilized during his march toward the city. If that supply line was cut off completely, Sherman thought, his army might find itself pressed, trapped in a Southern town, surrounded by the enemy. He sent a portion of his men north, under the command of General George Thomas, who had distinguished himself in battle several times throughout the war, to knock Hood's army out of the way.

In the meantime Sherman made a watershed decision. Rather than march back north, he would completely cut his supply line out of Chattanooga and lead his men on a campaign even deeper into Confederate territory. He decided to advance across Georgia, toward the port city of Savannah, and feed his men off the forced hospitality of the South. He wired his commander, General Ulysses S. Grant, who was already laying siege to Petersburg and the Confederate capital at Richmond. He informed Grant of his situation and of his plan to march across the state, destroying everything that represented a resource of war for the South. The war would be won, Sherman knew, only after the South's will to fight was crushed, and that will would only be destroyed when the

Confederacy's capacity to fight was eliminated. The Union commander was prepared to engage in total war—a strategy based on targeting civilian populations. Grant approved of Sherman's plan on November 2, sending him a telegram, as historian Allen Weinstein notes, that read: "I do not really see that you can withdraw from where you are to follow Hood [into Tennessee], without giving up all we have gained in territory. I say, then, go on as you propose."

Two weeks later Sherman was on the move, on that crisp fall day of November 16, ready to engage in a campaign that would gain him notoriety among Southerners, even as it might gain the Union the ultimate victory of the war—his March to the Sea. Before Sherman and his men were through they would cut a 60-mile (100-kilometer) wide swath of destruction across Georgia and beyond. Perhaps their work would help bring an end to the war. Perhaps the destruction would only further enflame Southerners to continue their fight.

Civil War America 1861–1865

Before the war began there were 19 free states—those that did not allow slavery. They were part of the Union. There were 15 slave states, forming the Confederacy. Delaware, Maryland, and Missouri were slave states but, when the war started, they fought for the Union. Kentucky considered itself neutral. West Virginia became a free state in 1863.

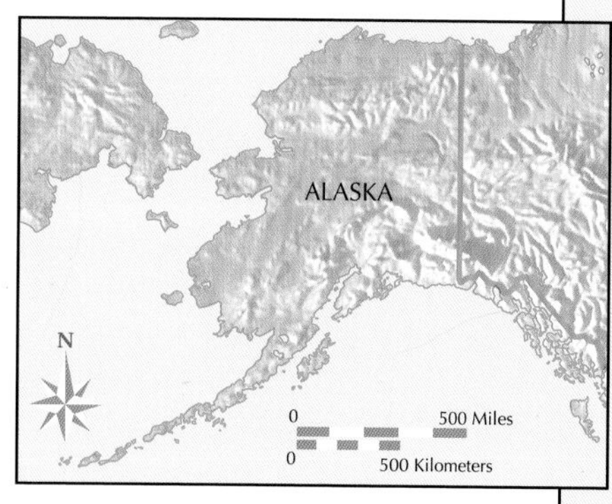

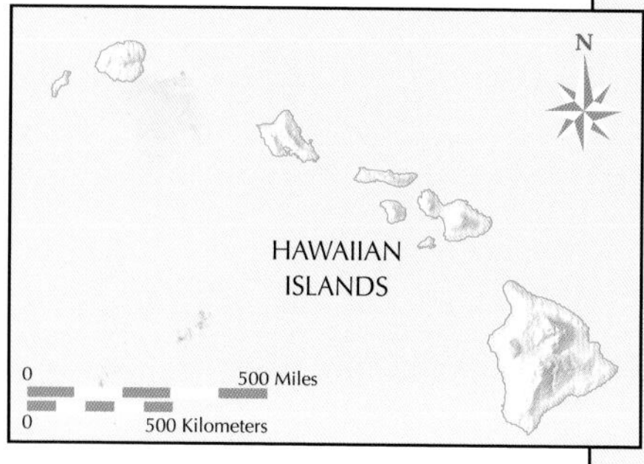

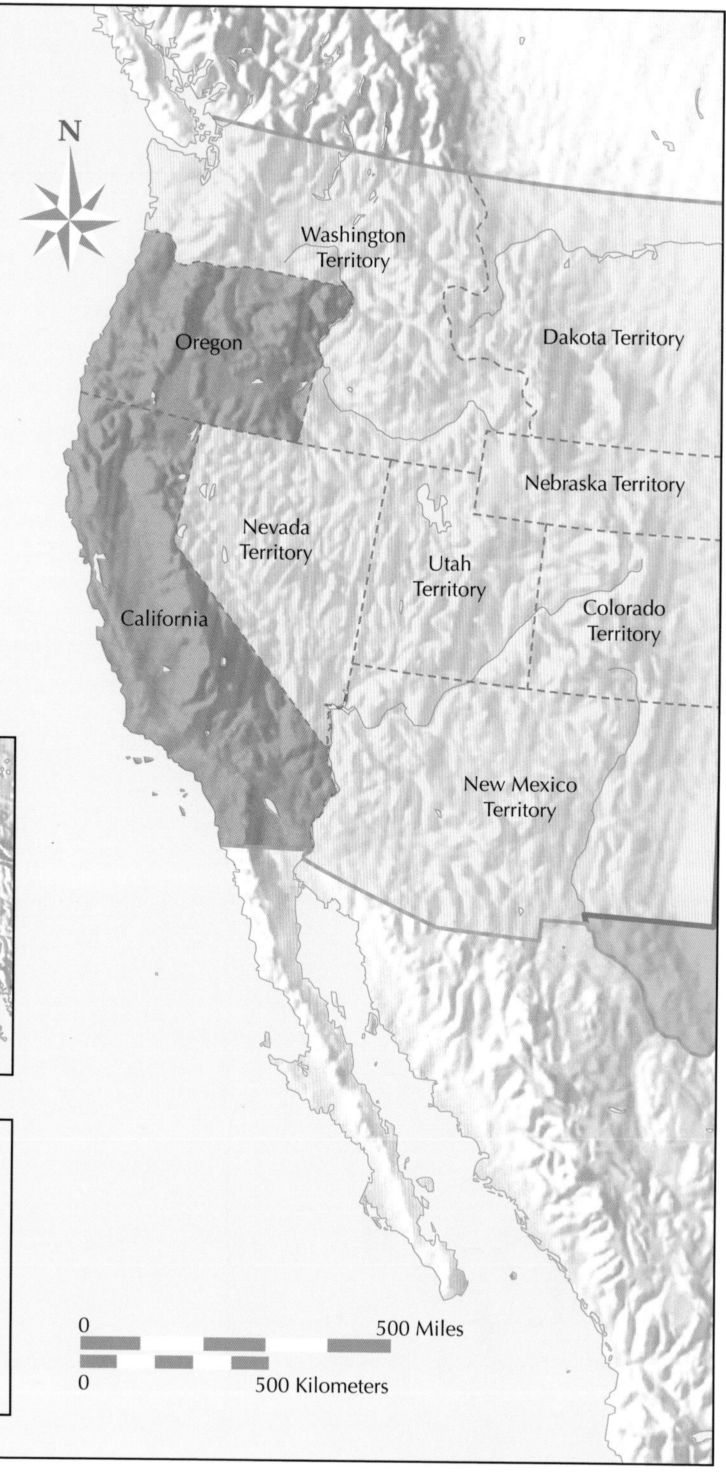

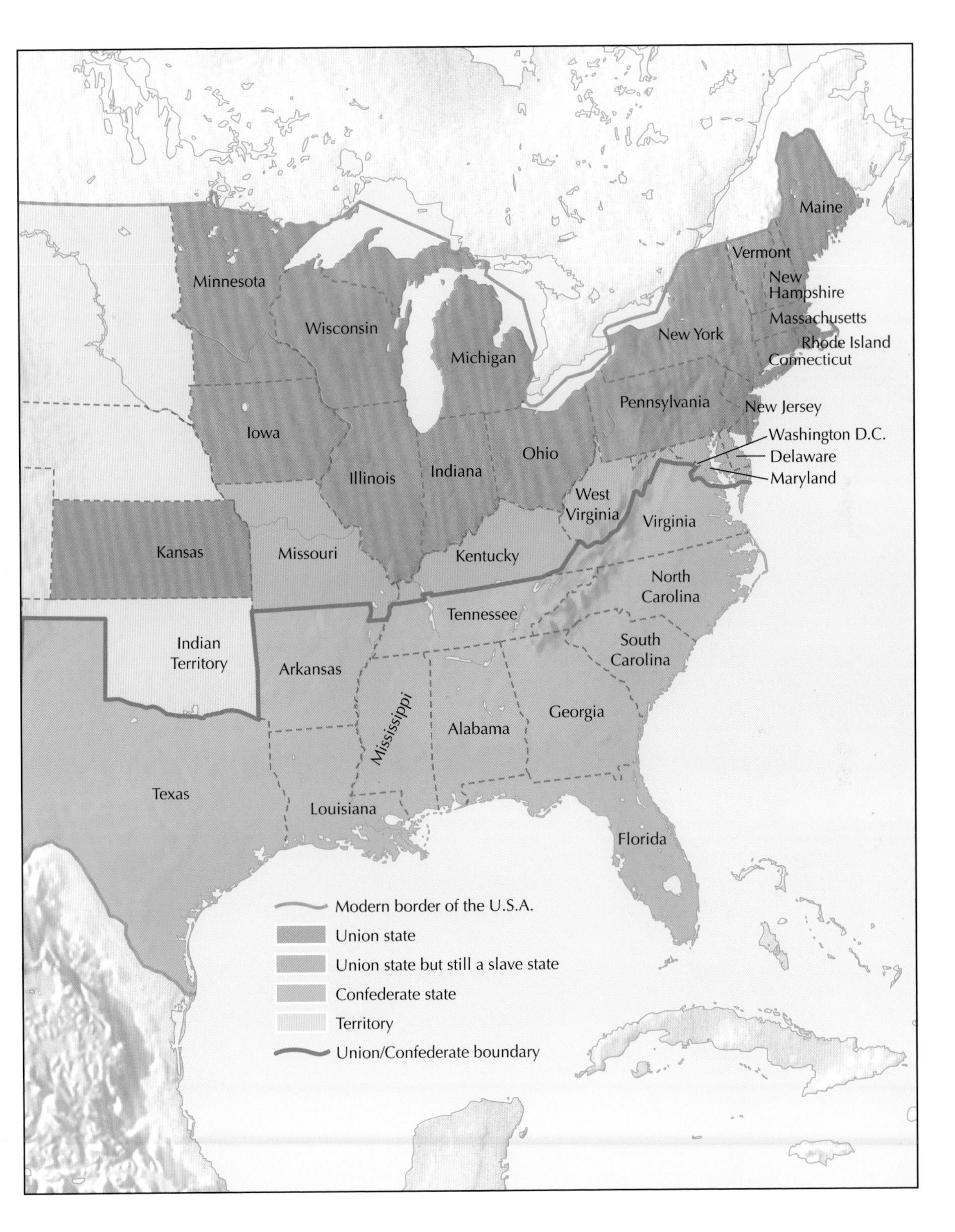

Maine
Vermont
New Hampshire
Massachusetts
Rhode Island
Connecticut
New York
Minnesota
Wisconsin
Michigan
Pennsylvania
New Jersey
Washington D.C.
Delaware
Maryland
Iowa
Ohio
Illinois
Indiana
West Virginia
Virginia
Kansas
Missouri
Kentucky
North Carolina
Tennessee
Indian Territory
Arkansas
South Carolina
Mississippi
Georgia
Alabama
Texas
Louisiana
Florida
Modern border of the U.S.A.
Union state
Union state but still a slave state
Confederate state
Territory
Union/Confederate boundary

1
A Challenge to Slavery

In 1860, the year Southern states began separating, or seceding, from the United States to form their own nation, many Americans saw their country through a different lens than today. They viewed the United States as a collection of several regions, including the North and South, and an ever-expanding West, which stretched across the Mississippi River, to the Rocky Mountains, and, finally, to the Pacific Ocean. California, as far to the west as one could travel by land, had become an American state a decade earlier. This geographic mindset was already partially in place when the country was established during the Revolutionary War (1775–83).

DIVIDING LINES

During the half century leading up to 1860 the divisions between the North and South had widened, and even hardened. The North had developed into a region of free people, where slavery could no longer be found. It was a world driven by commercial and industrial interests, as well as by the contributions made by countless thousands of prosperous family-owned farms. The northern landscape was dotted with tidy villages and small towns, containing shops, schools, public buildings, and churches. The South, by comparison, had remained a largely agricultural region. It was populated typically by small-time, yeoman farmers who eked out their livings in places that were sometimes still remote frontier lands, alongside a smaller, but powerful, class of wealthy planters who owned spreading plantations, manned by black slaves.

So much seemed so different when one compared life in the North to life in the South. Northerners spoke differently from Southerners, ate different foods, practiced different social customs, relied on different economic systems, had different habits, principles, and even manners. Each region had developed its own unique characteristics and ways of doing just about everything.

Even in the days of the American Revolution, people living in New England considered the Southern way of life as backward, Old World, and dependent on slavery. Meanwhile Southerners viewed their Northern counterparts as a distant, cold people, ruined by faceless city living, dependent on an underclass of workers paid low wages, their ranks filled with the poor and—even worse, some thought—immigrants. It was as if the United States was anything but united, as if the country contained two different and divergent peoples.

From time to time those regional differences had been placed on the back burner while the nation's people rallied on behalf of a common cause, such as the War of 1812 or the Mexican–American War. During such times patriotism had become the shared bond, creating a nationalistic feeling that animated Americans to work together. As the West opened up, a new generation of citizens moved into the open territo-

Wall Street, New York City, looking west toward Trinity Church on Broadway—a colored engraving of 1850. Grand financial buildings lined the sidewalks and horsedrawn omnibuses and carriages plied along the thoroughfare. Gas lamps lit the street at night.

ries, with the same intent—to occupy and settle those lands and together plant an American flag of progress.

Yet even this western movement of Americans ultimately worked to spread the cultural reach of both sections of the country, North and South. Northerners moved into the prairie lands of Illinois, Indiana, Michigan, and Wisconsin, where they built wheat and corn farms. Southerners, as they moved into modern-day Mississippi, Louisiana, Arkansas, and Texas, brought along their reliance on cotton cultivation and the slaves who worked those same fields. As slavery expanded, becoming a more lucrative labor system based on significant cotton profits, the breach between the parallel worlds of the Southerners and Northerners widened, creating great friction between the two regions.

There were other significant differences, as well. By the 1850s the North's population was half again as large as that of the South, and most of the nation's important cities—New York, Philadelphia, Boston, and Cincinnati—were Northern urban centers. Most of the new transportation systems, such as canals, railroads, and stagecoach lines, were also based in the North. Yet, at the core, the primary difference that symbolized the great gap between the two American regions was a single institution, one of labor and race—slavery.

THE WORLD OF THE SLAVES

Slavery in North America dated back to early in the colonial period. Blacks had been delivered to the Jamestown settlement in 1619, just 12 years after the founding of this British community. By a technicality of law, these early African arrivals were not officially slaves, but they were treated as such. By the 1660s statutes were drawn up in Virginia that began to define the institution of legal black slavery in America. However, the number of slaves did not increase dramatically until the early eighteenth century. In 1700 only

26,000 slaves were living in the British colonies of North America, but by 1775, the first year of the Revolutionary War, the slave population in the colonies stood at 500,000.

Despite the efforts of some patriot leaders, slavery survived the Revolution, even though its ideals were freedom, liberty, and equality. Yet the clash of arms with Great Britain and the formation of the new American Republic did have a dramatic impact on the scope of slavery in the colonies-turned-states. Northern states soon began bringing an end to slavery within their borders. Slave numbers in these states had never been significant, and the North had never developed an economic system dependent on slave labor. Pennsylvania banned slavery in 1780, with New Hampshire and Massachusetts following suit in 1783. Then Rhode Island and Connecticut did the same the following year, with New York and New Jersey joining their ranks in 1799 and 1804, respectively, as the last of the northern states to abolish slavery. In some of these states, slavery was ended on a gradual basis, with no new slaves being allowed and the children of slaves being free at birth. Slavery in such states was not completely done away with until the last slave died.

A Technological Boost

By the 1790s some Americans began to consider whether slavery would even continue in the Southern states. Profits on tobacco were falling off, causing the value of a slave to also drop. With no viable cash crop to support a slave labor system, how could slavery be expected to turn a profit? But the issue was settled almost as quickly as the question was raised. A Northerner named Eli Whitney invented his cotton engine, or "gin," which eliminated the bottleneck in the profitability of raising cotton across the South. With the cotton gin, a single slave could remove the sticky green seeds from cotton bolls. This task had previously held back the production of cotton, as it had required a vast amount of labor to "clean" the cotton bolls. Once again slavery could pay, so the institution was here to stay.

With the development of cotton production in the South, slavery produced great profits. As a result the value of slaves increased dramatically throughout the early 1800s. Between 1800 and 1860 the value of a prime slave field hand increased 20-fold. Cotton cultivation spread across the South, bursting out of the confines of the old, original states—Maryland, Virginia, the Carolinas, and Georgia—to the West, into Alabama, Mississippi, Louisiana, Texas, Arkansas, and western Tennessee. Perhaps no fact was more clear in the early decades of the nineteenth century than the new geographic face of slavery. It was no longer a national institution, but strictly a regional one—an essential part of the Southern economy and the old, entrenched Southern way of life.

A Slave's Work

For those blacks who were caught up in the infernal reach of slavery, life was precarious indeed. Of the 3.5 to 4 million slaves in the United States in 1860, approximately three out of four were put to work in the cotton fields. These slaves spent long days in the fields, bent over, hoeing out the weeds, a task referred to as "chopping cotton." At harvest time these same slaves—men and women alike—filed out into the same fields to continue stooping over the plants they had nurtured for almost six months, this time to pluck the cotton bolls that represented wealth and profits for those who owned the lands.

The slave's world was not of their making. They were property and were treated as such, with almost no rights recognized by white Southern society. Their lives were filled with long days of hard work, poverty, and sorrow. Slaves were treated paternalistically by their masters, as if they were children unable to take care of themselves. This attitude was prevalent and pervasive. The very act of owning slaves generally meant the owner was a racist, someone who did not believe that blacks were equal to whites in any way.

On a cotton plantation on Port Royal Island, South Carolina, in 1862, slaves prepare cotton bolls for the gin. This scene was repeated in much of the South and contrasted with "sophistication" in the North.

Everything was difficult for the slave. The typical slave diet was limited, generally including corn or cornmeal, fat pork or fish, molasses, and coffee. Slaves suffered from vitamin deficiencies, including scurvy and beriberi. They went shoeless, wore the same clothes all year, and lived in dirt-floor shacks that were hot in the summer and cold in the winter. They often shared such dwellings with other slave families. Every day was a workday; the only day the slave might not have to labor was Christmas Day.

This forced labor system included all sorts of other extremes. Slaves who refused to work were punished, often severely. Whippings were commonplace and were administered to the bare backs of both men and women, sometimes even to children. Other punishments included such cruelties as mutilation, burning and scalding, torture, and even murder. It was a system based on abuse. Yet, with the high profits from cotton, Southerners became even more reliant on large slave populations than before. There were other important Southern crops that provided the backbone of the region's agricultural economy, including tobacco, rice, sugar, and even hemp, but cotton, across the South, remained king.

THE MISSOURI COMPROMISE

This expansion of slavery became a heated issue, dividing North and South for decades prior to the Civil War. As Americans moved farther West, questions arose over whether slavery should be allowed to expand into these places. Such questions were often the topic of debate in Congress, where Northerners and Southerners argued over whether slavery or the labor of free men would dominate the lands west of the Mississippi River.

In 1819 a storm of concern swirled around just such a trans-Mississippi territory. Missouri applied to Congress to join the Union as a slave state. At question was whether or not the entire western region of the old Louisiana Purchase territory might be thrown open to slavery. Louisiana had already been admitted as a slave state, but that was clearly an extension into true Southern territory.

Complicating Missouri's request was the question of the balance of power in the Senate between slave and free states. In 1819 membership in the Senate was equally divided between 11 free and 11 slave states. To admit Missouri would tip the Senate majority in favor of the slave states. Long, heated debates ensued, and the issue was not decided until 1820. Kentucky Representative Henry Clay provided the answer through a compromise that allowed Missouri to enter the Union with slavery, while another territory, Maine, became a new free state. Thus, the balance between slave and free was maintained, at least for the moment. But the compromise included another clause: Clay proposed that future slave states carved out of the former Louisiana Territory would be limited to those lying south of Missouri's southern border, a line of 36 degrees, 30 minutes north latitude. North of that line, slavery would be prohibited, since such states would, by definition, fit the same geography as the North.

A true crisis had been averted, but slavery had advanced farther west. As noted by historian Robert Remini, a New Hampshire representative lamented: "The Southern & Western people talked so much, threatened so loudly, & predicted such dreadful consequences... that they fairly frightened our weak-minded members into an abandonment of their stand against slavery in the territories." At the center of these arguments over the extension of slavery into the West was the question of whether Congress even had the power or authority to determine where slavery should or should not be planted. Southerners claimed the Constitution did not provide such congressional power, while Northerners noted that Congress had already assumed that power. During the 1780s, under the earlier Articles of Confederation, Congress had barred slavery from the Northwest Territory (today's Ohio, Indiana, Illinois, Michigan, and Wisconsin). In 1798 Congress had discussed prohibiting slavery in the Mississippi Territory (today's Alabama and Mississippi states). This question of congressional power over slavery's advance would remain a hotbed issue for decades to follow.

THE ABOLITIONISTS

While Southerners generally gave their support to slavery, most Northerners, at the time of the Missouri Compromise, were not actually opposed to the institution. The people of the North may have decided to abolish slavery in their own states, but that did not translate to their opposition to slavery across the South. The vast majority of Americans in the early nineteenth century did not believe blacks to be equal to whites, and many in the North were largely apathetic about slavery as it existed in the South. But by the time of the Missouri Compromise a reform movement was afoot, based in the North, that questioned not just the expansion of slavery, but its very existence. The reformers were generally referred to as abolitionists—those who supported the abolition, or termination, of the enslavement of hundreds of thousands of black men, women, and children.

William Lloyd Garrison

One of the leading abolitionists, and one of the loudest, was William Lloyd Garrison. By the 1820s Garrison was writing for an anti-slave newspaper in Baltimore, named *The Genius of Universal Emancipation.* Then in 1831 Garrison, just a young man in his late twenties, began publishing his own abolitionist paper, *The Liberator.* In the paper's first issue, dated January 1, Garrison threw down the gauntlet:

In Park Street Church, on the Fourth of July, 1829, in an address on slavery, I [thoughtlessly agreed] to the popular but pernicious doctrine of gradual abolition. I seize this opportunity to make a full... recantation.

I will be as harsh as truth, and as uncompromising as justice. On this subject, I do not wish to think, or speak, or write with moderation... I am in earnest—I will not equivocate—I will not excuse—I will not retreat a single inch—AND I WILL BE HEARD.

Indeed, few American voices in opposition to the institution of slavery would prove more enduring and effective than that of William Lloyd Garrison. He published *The Liberator* for nearly 35 years, through the Civil War, until Congress finally abolished slavery in 1865.

Garrison's campaign did not have an instant effect on the issues of the day. His paper was not immediately popular, and early copies did not sell well. During his first year of publishing *The Liberator* in Boston's Merchants' Hall, he changed offices four times to pay less rent. He often worked 14-hour days, slept on an office table, and relied on a cake and fruit shop in the building's basement for food. Garrison's lack of popularity was due, not only to his call for "immediatism" in freeing the slaves, but to his insistence on racial equality for all blacks in the United States.

Abolitionists such as Garrison did not generally take up weapons in opposition to slavery, but instead wielded the pen. They relied on "moral suasion," to convince their audience that slavery was immoral, an absolute wrong against humanity that could not be excused or justified. They described slaveholding as a sin, a practice that denied blacks their "unalienable rights," as Jefferson had described them in the *Declaration of Independence*. The vast majority of the people the abolitionists addressed were Northerners. Most

Southerners were rarely exposed to the messages of those calling for slavery's immediate end.

"A Positive Good"

One influential Southerner who did respond to Garrison's abolitionist message was John C. Calhoun. A former senator from South Carolina, Calhoun had served as Andrew Jackson's vice president between 1829 and 1833. He became an outspoken advocate and apologist for slavery, as seen in a speech in Congress in 1837:

Whose Slaves Were They?

Prior to the American Civil War, no other institution explained the difference between life in the North and South better than slavery. Slavery in the North had largely been eliminated before or just after 1800. In the same period the institution survived and dramatically increased in scope across the South, with the invention of the cotton gin and the development of a cotton-based farming economy. Cotton became such an important export in the United States that its sales accounted for 50 percent of all exports in 1860. Yet, while slavery partially defined the South during the first half of the nineteenth century, many Southerners did not own slaves at all.

When the Civil War began in 1861 the total white population of the South was some 7 million people, representing around 1.4 million households. Yet, of that number, only about 383,000 households owned slaves. So three out of every four white families in the South did *not* own any slaves, and many of those who were slaveowners owned only one or two. In all, fewer than 48,000 slave-holders owned 20 slaves or more. (Twenty was the benchmark number for a slaveowner to be considered a member of the more elite "planter" class.) Thus, while hundreds of thousands of white men fought for the Confederacy during the Civil War, most did not own slaves.

I hold that in the present state of civilization, where two races of different origin, and distinguished by color and other physical differences, as well as intellectual, are brought together, the relation now existing in the slaveholding states between the two is, instead of an evil, a good—a positive good.

Men such as Calhoun—including ministers, lawyers, philosophers, doctors, politicians, and other professionals—justified slavery without apology. Blacks were inferior, they argued, so slavery was a means of providing them with work, the basic necessities of life, and security. They claimed blacks were content, even happy, as slaves. Ministers declared from their pulpits that God himself had determined that blacks should be held as slaves.

A VOLATILE DECADE

The 1830s proved a decade of change for the abolitionist movement. By 1832 William Lloyd Garrison had organized the New England Antislavery Society and in the following year he set up a national organization, the American Antislavery Society. By the decade's end, this national group had 2,000 local chapters and a membership of 200,000. Those opposed to the radicalism of Garrison and his followers believed that the abolitionists only stirred up animosity and encouraged slaves to revolt. They blamed Garrison for a slave uprising in 1831, led by a Virginia slave named Nat Turner, in which 57 whites, including women and children were killed. There was in fact probably no connection.

In the fall of 1834, in Philadelphia, an antiabolitionist riot destroyed 45 black homes. The next year a mob nearly hanged Garrison in Boston. The U.S. Postmaster General even banned all antislavery literature from mail delivered in the South, fearing that such writings would land in the hands of blacks. In Congress, the House of Representatives established a "gag order" on even discussing slavery, which remained in place between 1836 and 1844.

In the fall of 1837 a mob shot and killed an antislavery newspaper publisher, the Reverend Elijah P. Lovejoy, outside a warehouse in Alton, Illinois. Lovejoy had gone to the warehouse to protect his new printing press, since he had lost several presses to earlier attacks by proslavery groups. The death of Reverend Lovejoy sent a shock wave across the country. A white mob had killed a white minister in a free state over slavery. Historian David Brion Davis notes that Garrison addressed the killing in *The Liberator,* writing, "When we first unfurled the banner of *The Liberator,* we did not anticipate that... free states would voluntarily trample underfoot all order, law, and government, or brand the advocates of universal liberty as incendiaries."

In the weeks following the Lovejoy killing, a minister in a Congregational church in Hudson, Ohio, delivered a sermon in which he spoke of the mob action. He asked, as noted by historian Geoffrey Ward: "The question now before us is no longer can slaves be made free, but are we free or are we slaves under mob law?" At the sermon's end, a thin man rose from his pew, raised his right hand, and swore before the assembled congregation: "Here, before God, in the presence of these witnesses, I consecrate my life to the destruction of slavery." The haggard, quiet man in his mid-thirties, was destined to become, over the next 20 years, one of the country's most passionate, yet violent, opponents of slavery—John Brown.

2 Slavery and Politics

During the early 1840s slavery continued to divide Americans. In 1844, former President John Quincy Adams, then a member of the House of Representatives, repealed the gag order against slavery discussions. Then, in 1846, the United States went to war with Mexico over a border dispute. In August, before most of the war had been fought, House members considered a bill to appropriate $2 million to help the transfer of Mexican territory to the United States. Americans were already certain they would win the war and that the government would gain territory from Mexico. The bill would probably not have raised much controversy, except for an amendment that stated, "neither slavery nor involuntary servitude shall ever exist in any part of said territory."

POPULAR SOVEREIGNTY

The amendment, though not passed, raised an immediate howl. But the issue of slavery in new American territories remained in the air. Month after month the amendment came up, only to be passed in the House and shunned by the Senate. The war ended in 1847 and the following year the United States did gain land, stretching from California to Texas, which, for the moment, was open to the advance of slavery. As had been the case for years, debate over slavery's movement west continued to center on whether Congress had the power to limit its expansion. But a new theory was introduced by the late 1840s, which sought to bypass that thorny question. It was a political view called "popular sovereignty," one thrashed out by two Democrat senators from the North—Stephen Douglas of Illinois and Lewis Cass of Michigan.

The idea of popular sovereignty was simple, and compelling to many Americans. Why not respect the American tradition of local self-government and allow the residents of a territory to decide for themselves whether or not they wanted slavery in their future state? The issue made the question of congressional power moot. Cass had the opportunity to advance his view in 1848, when he was nominated as the Democrat candidate for president. Yet the party placed in its platform a plank stating that Congress did not have the power to limit the expansion of slavery. Democrats had to walk a thin line on these issues, since they had supporters in both the North and South.

That position caused some Northern Democrats to break from the party. They nominated former President Martin Van Buren, a New Yorker who opposed slavery, as their candidate under the banner of the newly formed Free Soil party. The Free-Soilers gained support from abolitionist Whigs and Democrats, as well as old Liberty Party supporters. (The Liberty Party had been formed in 1840, and had supported an antislavery candidate, James Birney, in both the 1840 and 1844 elections. Birney only received 7,000 and 62,000 votes, respectively, ending the party's run.) The Free Soil Party drafted a slogan, calling for "free soil, free speech, free labor, and free men."

The Whig Party tried to skirt the real issues by running a hero from the Mexican–American War, General Zachary Taylor. The general managed a victory, taking 163 electoral votes to Cass's 127. The popular vote—1.36 million for Taylor and 1.22 million for Cass—was close, but Van Buren ruined Cass's possibilities of a win by taking away almost 300,000 votes (and with them, the state of New York) for himself. While Taylor would likely have supported the spread of slavery into the West, he did not have much of an impact on events. He died in office on July 9, 1850, from an acute attack of gastroenteritis, brought on by eating uncooked vegetables and cherries washed down by a large quantity of buttermilk.

THE COMPROMISE OF 1850

Taylor's death took place in the midst of yet another swirl of controversy. The acquisition of California from Mexico coincided with the discovery of gold in the northern portion of the territory. By 1849 thousands of would-be prospectors were arriving in San Francisco and Sacramento, seeking their fortunes. This great influx of Forty-Niners caused California's population to zoom from 6,000 to over 85,000, enough people to allow Californians to meet in September to draft a constitution, in which they outlawed slavery. Skipping the establishment of a territorial government, a draft was sent to Congress for immediate statehood. At that time, President Taylor had been prepared to bring California, as well as New Mexico, into the Union as slave states. Bitter arguments reverberated in the halls of Congress. Northerners and Southerners both dug in, both determined to make California a testing ground for slavery's future in the West.

The Barrel Machine Room in an E. Remington & Sons' armory in New York in about 1860. The factory was one of many set up in the North.

Once again, Kentuckian Henry Clay, now 73 years old, cobbled together a complicated compromise, which he proposed on January 29, 1850. The package included: the admission of California as a state with no reference to slavery (California would, indeed, remain a free state); the establishment of the New Mexico and Utah territories, with popular sovereignty to determine slavery's future there; the settlement of a border dispute between Texas and New Mexico and the federal assumption of $10 million in Texas public debt; the abolition of the slave trade in Washington, D.C.; and a stronger fugitive slave law. With the compromise including something for everyone, it was accepted. (During the debates that spring, the aged John C. Calhoun died, his body racked with tuberculosis.)

Once again, the nation had steered clear of an absolute crisis, but perhaps no other political compromise has had a greater impact on U.S. history than the Compromise of 1850. The agreement made it possible for the country to escape dissolution and civil war for another decade. During those ten years, the Northern states experienced a period of rapid industrial growth and development, with new inventions and innovations, as well as factories, railroads, mines, and mills. When the Civil War did arrive, this industrial base would provide the machinery of war that the North needed to defeat the Confederate states. Also, the decade of the 1850s would see the rise of Abraham Lincoln to political notice and ultimately, political power. Ultimately he would become president, and the leader responsible for seeing the Union through the war.

A NEW DECADE OF CONFLICT

Throughout the next few years, the nation avoided general political crisis. Then, in 1852, the daughter of one of the most outspoken antislavery ministers in New England,

135,000 SETS, 270,000 VOLUMES SOLD.

UNCLE TOM'S CABIN

FOR SALE HERE.

AN EDITION FOR THE MILLION, COMPLETE IN 1 Vol., PRICE 37 1-2 CENTS.
" " IN GERMAN, IN 1 Vol., PRICE 50 CENTS.
" " IN 2 Vols., CLOTH, 6 PLATES, PRICE $1.50.
SUPERB ILLUSTRATED EDITION, IN 1 Vol., WITH 153 ENGRAVINGS,
PRICES FROM $2.50 TO $5.00.

The Greatest Book of the Age.

An advertisement for Harriet Beecher Stowe's novel. *Uncle Tom's Cabin* told the story of Tom, a long-suffering slave, who rescues a white girl, but then is sold to a sadistic plantation owner who finally has him killed.

Harriet Beecher Stowe, wrote an antislavery novel called *Uncle Tom's Cabin; or Life Among the Lowly*. It soon became one of the most important books in American history. For perhaps the first time, someone had written in opposition to slavery through a compelling use of fiction. Stowe's characters included black slaves with whom the reader could feel true sympathy, even empathy.

Stowe's portrayal of slavery persuaded people who had never considered seriously the wrongs of the institution to take a closer look and conclude that slavery had no place in America. The book also served as an indictment of the new fugitive slave law, included in the Compromise of 1850, which required Northern law enforcement officials to assist in the recovery of slaves who escaped into a free state or territory. Stowe's book was an immediate bestseller, with a million copies sold by mid-1853.

The Kansas–Nebraska Act

In the meantime the election of 1852 delivered a smashing victory to the New Hampshire Democrat, Franklin Pierce. During Pierce's term harmony between the North and South continued to unravel, with the introduction of a controversial bill in Congress by Illinois Senator Stephen Douglas. The Kansas–Nebraska bill, passed in May 1854, was intended to organize the two northern territories of Kansas and Nebraska. In structuring both territories, Douglas included the element of popular sovereignty. Since the Missouri Compromise of 1820 had banned slavery north of Missouri's southern border, this new legislation destroyed the 34-year-old agreement, and technically opened those lands to possible slavery. For Southerners who supported the bill, the expectation was that Kansas would become a slave state and Nebraska a free state. But the Kansas–Nebraska Act also destroyed the relative peace that had existed in Congress since the passage of the Compromise of 1850, and that peace would never be reinstated before the coming of the Civil War.

The act had other direct political impacts, such as the collapse of the Whig Party and the formation of a new political group from its ashes. On February 24, 1854, even before the Kansas–Nebraska bill was fully passed, several former Free-Soilers, Northern Whigs, and abolitionist Democrats met in Ripon, Wisconsin, and formed a new political party, the Republicans. After the Kansas–Nebraska Act became law, they—and hundreds of thousands of others—demanded the repeal of the act and of the Fugitive Slave Act of 1850.

Revenge and Retribution

Douglas watched the following fall as his Kansas–Nebraska Act led to the ouster of several fellow Democrats from Congress. Meanwhile, with Kansas now thrown open to slavery, both anti-slave and pro-slave supporters rushed out to the territory, hoping to sway the direction of the decision over slavery's future in Kansas. When an election was held in 1855 thousands of proslavery men from Missouri came across the border to vote in Kansas, with the result that Kansas soon saw the formation of a proslavery legislature, even though the majority of Kansans were opposed to slavery. In response, antislavery men called a convention of their own and illegally created their own government and constitution. Animosity grew. Clashes between the two groups led to the violent event that became known as "Bleeding Kansas."

During the second half of the 1850s, perhaps as many as 200 people on both sides were killed over the slave issue. After a proslavery posse sacked the town of Lawrence, Kansas, killing several Free-Soilers in cold blood, John Brown and a half dozen or so of his sons carried out an act of revenge against a proslavery settlement at Potawatomie Creek. There Brown, his boys, and several other followers pulled five proslavery men from their cabins out into the night and hacked them to death with broadswords, stringing their intestines out over the cold Kansas prairie. In return proslavery men attacked Brown's settlement at Osawatomie, burning cabins and killing several people, including one of Brown's sons. At that point, federal troops were called in.

VIOLENCE IN THE SENATE

The violence over slavery even extended back East, into the very halls of Congress. On May 19, 1856, Charles Sumner, an abolitionist senator from Massachusetts, delivered a speech titled "The Crime Against Kansas." As noted by historian Geoffrey Ward, Sumner called border-jumping Missourians "hirelings picked from the drunken spew and vomit of an uneasy civilization" for invading Kansas to alter the outcome of the vote on slavery. In his bitter diatribe Sumner was critical of a fellow senator, Andrew Pickens Butler, a proslavery supporter from South Carolina. Sumner even made fun of Butler's speech impediment during his presentation.

During the speech Butler had not been present in the room. Three days later Butler's nephew, Representative Preston Brooks, caught Sumner at his desk between sessions in the Senate Chamber and proceeded to beat him on the head with his gold-headed wooden cane. The walking stick broke to pieces only after cracking Sumner's skull. During the assault, an associate of Brooks, Laurence M. Keitt, also from South Carolina, held a pistol on other senators who tried to rush to Sumner's aid. Brooks nearly killed Sumner that day—the Massachusetts senator was three years recuperating from his wounds, and never fully recovered. Just as in Kansas, violence over slavery had reared its ugly head.

Preston Brooks resigned his House seat after his attack on Sumner, yet the people of his South Carolina district reelected him. He did not live to see any retribution for his actions against the Massachusetts senator, as he died five months later of a liver disease. The national crisis was reaching epic proportions that year, and the country was in desperate need of a forceful chief executive.

THE DRED SCOTT CASE

James Buchanan, a Democrat from Pennsylvania, had been elected president in 1856, but he did not prove to be a decisive voice in the American sea of crisis and confrontation. Buchanan even suggested at his Inaugural that the Supreme

JOHN BROWN: THE LIFE OF AN ABOLITIONIST

Throughout the first 50 years of his life, the abolitionist John Brown managed to remain an unknown. But his dedication to destroying slavery by any means would eventually make his a household name in mid-nineteenth century America.

Brown was born in Connecticut in 1800 and grew up on the frontier of Ohio. His parents raised him to love the Scriptures and hate slavery. All through his life John Brown struggled with failure. When he could not make a go of farming, he tried several business ventures as a tanner, land speculator, shepherd, and wool merchant—all of which failed miserably. As a result his large family of 20 children was typically poor.

Even as Brown tried to find a suitable means of making a living, he became passionate about one thing—his hatred of slavery and his attraction to the abolitionist movement. For several years this translated itself into simple, low-key actions. He taught his children about the evils of slavery. He attended churches where he and his family might sit next to black worshipers. One of his daughters, Ruth, remembered as an adult being asked by her father if she would be willing to share her food and clothing with some poor black children he wanted to take in to live with his family.

Then, in 1837, Brown's support of abolitionism took a decided turn. He

Court was on the verge of handing down a ruling that would settle the slavery question once and for all. That ruling was the *Dred Scott v. Sandford* case, and the Court's decision in this case would prove one of the most important, if misplaced, decisions in American history. The background to the case was simple: Dred Scott was a slave who had sued for his freedom, on the grounds that he had been taken by a previous owner to live in a free state (Illinois) several years earlier and then into a free territory (today's Minnesota). Dred Scott's claim was that while he lived in those places he

dedicated himself to the destruction of slavery following the murder by proslavery Illinoisians of an abolitionist minister in Alton. Perhaps Brown's own poverty and lower class status as a white man helped him to develop an empathy with oppressed blacks, both free and slave. For Brown, money was always short and feeding his family was difficult. He was poor and he was painfully aware of it. He may have come to identify with the plight of many blacks, and thought he shared in their miseries. He even moved to live for two years in a community of freed blacks in North Elba, New York.

Once Brown dedicated himself to the destruction of slavery, he took bold and overt steps against the institution and its supporters. He became a "conductor" on the Underground Railroad, the secret system of safe houses that runaway Southern slaves could follow to Northern freedom. He formed a self-protection league for free blacks.

Brown was driven in his fight against slavery by his Christian beliefs. To him, the Scriptures spoke loudly about slavery. His favorite verse was in the New Testament book of Hebrews, Chapter 9, Verse 22: "Without the shedding of blood, there is no remission of sins." In Brown's mind, the sin of slavery would have to be purged with blood. Thus, when Kansas exploded in violence between slave-holders and antislavery supporters, Brown would find himself in their midst, ready to kill in the name of eradicating slavery.

became free, since slavery was barred there. The case had already gone through two Missouri courts before landing in the lap of the Supreme Court.

The Court's majority decision determined that Scott did not have the right to sue in Court, since he was not a citizen of the United States, and that the Constitution offered no rights to blacks that any white man was bound to recognize. The Court also announced that the Missouri Compromise had been unconstitutional.

Buchanan had been wrong in thinking that the Dred Scott decision would settle the slavery question. In fact the decision only managed to further rile Northerners, since the case seemed to indicate that slavery could not be barred from anywhere and that Southerners were free to take their slaves wherever they might choose.

FURTHER DIVISIONS

Congress exploded. Debates became fistfights. On one occasion a brawl broke out that involved 50 House members wrestling with one another on the House floor. During the fight a Wisconsin representative, John F. "Bowie Knife" Potter, yanked off the toupee of Mississippi's William Barksdale. Historian Robert Remini recalls Potter shouting: "I've scalped him!" which caused the House to break out in uproarious laughter.

Yet events were becoming more desperate. Stephen Douglas found himself in a terrible bind, as his "popular sovereignty" was no longer valid. In addition he offended Southern Democrats in 1857, when he refused to accept a proposed territorial constitution submitted by Kansas that allowed for slavery. Buchanan accepted it wholeheartedly and tried to shove it through Congress. It was clear to Douglas that the majority will of the people of Kansas was that the territory be established as free.

The Underground Railroad

People that helped slaves escape to the North set up several special routes for the slaves to follow. Along each route was a series of secret hiding places. The combination of helpers and hiding places formed what became known as the "underground railroad." Safe houses were referred to as "stations," and their owners as "station masters." One of the most famous guides or "conductors" was Harriet Tubman, a slave from a Maryland plantation who escaped to Pennsylvania and, over a period of 10 years, helped more than 300 slaves escape to freedom.

Exhausted slaves are hustled by conductors to a hiding place in a barn as slave-catchers pursue the runaways.

Then, in 1858, Douglas faced a new Republican challenger during his reelection bid for the Senate. Abraham Lincoln had already begun to make a name for himself in Illinois, and the Republicans tapped him to take on the political giant. The two men engaged in a series of seven now-famous debates, scattered across the state, in which they both offered their views on popular sovereignty, the Missouri Compromise, the future of slavery, the Dred Scott decision, and every other important issue related to slavery. They were rousing, well-attended debates, with Lincoln taking the opportunity during the contest in Freeport, Illinois, to ask Douglas a tough question: Given the Dred Scott decision, how could the doctrine of popular sovereignty have any meaning any longer? In other words, if the Dred Scott decision allowed a slaveowner to take his slaves anywhere of his choosing, how could the people of a given territory vote slavery up or down?

Douglas stood to lose, regardless of his answer. He responded, admitting that slavery could not "exist a day or an hour anywhere, unless it was supported by local police regulations," notes historian Remini. Douglas was admitting that no slaveowner would dare take his slave where there were not strong black codes in place. His answer could not help but offend Southerners and ensured that they would never support Douglas for president. While Douglas won his Senate seat, Lincoln was catapulted onto the national stage.

The End of John Brown

The following year old John Brown again entered the national spotlight. Along with a small group of both black and white followers, he engaged in a plot to raid the federal arsenal at Harper's Ferry, Virginia (today part of West Virginia), located 50 miles (80 km) from Washington, D.C. They intended to gather up a cache of weapons, with which they would arm local slaves and foment a general slave rebellion. Brown imagined that their efforts would have a ripple effect and bring down the institution of slavery altogether.

Brown and his men launched their uprising on the night of October 16, but almost immediately everything went wrong. Several of Brown's men were killed, and Brown himself was taken prisoner after a counter-raid by U.S. Marines, led by Colonel Robert E. Lee, who would soon become one of the most famous generals of the Civil War. Brown was hanged on December 2, 1859. Some Americans rejoiced at his death, while others mourned the passing of a fervent abolitionist.

THE ELECTION OF 1860

Just four months later Democrats met in Charleston, South Carolina, to choose their candidate for president. The convention immediately revealed the splits dividing the party. Northerners were unprepared to support the unlimited expansion of slavery across the West, which caused eight Southern state delegations to walk out. Issues concerning slavery had finally rent the party in two. Northern Democrats plunged ahead and met in Baltimore at their own convention in June, where they nominated Stephen Douglas as their candidate, with Herschel V. Johnson from Georgia as his running mate. Southerners also met in Baltimore at a convention less than two weeks later, and selected John Breckinridge from Kentucky and Joseph Lane of Oregon as their presidential and vice presidential candidates. In both cases the two factions chose both a Northerner and a Southerner for their dual tickets.

When Republicans met at their convention in Chicago on May 16, the selection of a candidate seemed up in the air. New York Senator William H. Seward had appeared to many Republicans as the most viable candidate, until he had delivered a controversial speech in October 1858. Speaking in Rochester, New York, Seward had predicted the future of the slave controversy, as noted by historian Doris Kearns Goodwin:

> *It is an irrepressible conflict between opposing and enduring forces, and it means that the United States must and will, sooner or later, become either entirely a slaveholding nation, or entirely a free-labor nation.*

This speech had been applauded by abolitionists and condemned by Southerners, yet many Northerners, including Republicans, were frightened by it. Ironically, Abraham Lincoln had expressed a similar expectation concerning slavery's future in America, in his now-famous "House Divided" speech, delivered in June 1858:

> *I believe this government cannot endure permanently, half slave and half free. I do not expect the Union to be dissolved—I do not expect the House to fall—but I do expect it to cease to be divided. It will become all one thing or all the other.*

But Lincoln had avoided the term "conflict" and had attempted a call for understanding and reconciliation between North and South. Lincoln had delivered a more recent speech, in February 1860, at New York City's Cooper Union, which had been even more conciliatory:

> *Let us do nothing through passion and ill temper. Even though the southern people will not so much as listen to us, let us calmly consider their demand, and yield to them if, in our deliberate view of our duty, we possibly can.*

Lincoln's words helped him to receive his party's nomination on the third ballot, along with Hannibal Hamlin as his running mate. He went on to win the election on November 6, taking 18 Northern (and free) states with 180 electoral votes. Out in Springfield, Illinois, an excited Lincoln received the news of his election by telegraph. But the challenges before him soon met his eye, and he recalled later how he "began at once to feel that I needed support, others to share with me the burden." Lincoln did not know at the time just how extensive his burdens would really become.

3

From Fort Sumter to Bull Run

Events moved quickly following Lincoln's election in November 1860. On December 20, before Lincoln had even been sworn in as president, South Carolinians passed an ordinance of secession, separating their state, as noted by historian Robert Remini, from all others "comprising the United States of America." This political separation was accompanied by war whoops and excited cheering. Other Southern states soon followed suit: Mississippi (January 9, 1861), Florida (January 10), Alabama (January 11), Georgia (January 19), Louisiana (January 26), and Texas (February 1), despite pleas from an aged Sam Houston that they should not leave the Union.

THE FOUNDING OF THE CONFEDERACY

The breakaway states established a new government—the Confederate States of America—and met in their new capital at Montgomery, Alabama, on February 8. A constitution was drawn up, very similar to the U.S. Constitution, but recognizing state sovereignty, protecting the institution of slavery, and providing a six-year term for their new country's president, Jefferson Davis, a former U.S. Senator and Secretary of War, and vice president, Alexander Stephens. Eight other slave states did not immediately secede. They remained watchful, uncertain whether the future would lead to war or not. Virginia, North Carolina, Tennessee, and Arkansas decided not to join the Confederacy unless war started.

In the meantime, lameduck President James Buchanan did nothing significant. Some steps were taken by Congress to stave off the possibility of war and further separation. A peace convention was held in Washington on February 4, with former President John Tyler presiding over the secret meeting. But those attending could not reach any acceptable point of compromise. Three weeks later Congress attempted to amend the Constitution to protect slavery in states where it already existed. The amendment passed both the House and Senate, but the states refused to ratify it. Less than a week later, Abraham Lincoln was sworn in as President of the United States.

Lincoln's Vain Attempt

In his Inaugural Address, Lincoln spoke directly to Southerners, reminding them of the common history all Americans shared and stating that he had no intention of interfering with slavery where it already existed. As historian Geoffrey Ward notes, Lincoln assured the South that he would not make overt moves toward war:

> *In your hands, my dissatisfied fellow countrymen, and not in mine, is the momentous issue of civil war... We are not enemies, but friends. We must not be enemies. Though passion may have strained, it must not break the bonds of affection.*

The mystic chords of memory, stretching from every battle-field and patriot grave, to every living heart and hearth-stone, all over this broad land, will yet swell the chorus of the Union, when again touched, as surely they will be, by the better angels of our nature.

Lincoln's words fell on deaf ears.

THE WAR BEGINS

One of Lincoln's practical problems when he took office was what to do about federal property in states that had seceded from the Union. There were military installations, forts, levees, and lighthouses scattered across the South. The most

THE GEOGRAPHY OF WAR

The battles of the Civil War would be fought from New Mexico to Pennsylvania, across many different forms of terrain. Looking at a map, the Confederate states were, generally, surrounded by water, including the Atlantic Ocean to the east, the Gulf of Mexico to the south, and the Ohio River along the north. The Mississippi River to the west divided the Confederacy from the western states of Arkansas, Louisiana, and Texas.

In the interior land east of the Mississippi, mountains and rolling hills split the Confederate states even further. The Appalachian Mountains stretch from the northeast to the southwest, cutting Virginia and North Carolina from Tennessee and northern Georgia and Alabama.

Fighting would occur in several regions throughout the war, but Virginia witnessed the most battles. Some engagements took place in the coastal lands of the tidewater where low-lying swamps made moving armies difficult. At least a dozen rivers—including the Potomac, James, York, Rappahannock, Appomattox, and Chickahominy—sliced across the state from the Appalachians to the pressing was Fort Sumter, a newly constructed masonry fort on an island in Charleston Harbor, South Carolina.

That spring the fort was short of food and supplies, and on April 4 Lincoln informed the governor of South Carolina by telegram that he intended to resupply the small garrison stationed there. President Davis ordered the fort evacuated. When the fort's commander, Major John Anderson, refused, Confederate coastal batteries opened fire on the fort at 4:30 A.M. on April 12, 1861. Ironically, the Confederate commander who ordered the artillery barrage, P.G.T. Beauregard, had studied artillery under Anderson at West Point. Anderson and his men held out for most of two days, then surrendered on April 14. The Civil War had finally begun.

Chesapeake Bay, also impeding army movements.

In the western portion of Virginia, the Piedmont country rose slowly toward the Appalachians. Between singular spines of hills lay fertile valleys, which provided food for Confederate armies. The most important was the Shenandoah Valley. Situated west of the Blue Ridge, and known simply as "the Valley," the Shenandoah was highly valued by the Confederacy. It was home to some of the South's richest grain fields, providing the Confederacy's breadbasket. The valley's Blue Ridge also provided cover for Rebel troop movements.

While Virginia was a constant battlefield, other Southern states also saw their share of action. Tennessee and Georgia witnessed significant fighting. In eastern Tennessee and northern Georgia, troops had to move around steep mountains. In other areas, such as Louisiana, South Carolina, and Mississippi, the fighting took place in flat, piney woods. Some secessionist states, including Texas, Arkansas, Alabama, North Carolina, and Florida, saw little action during the war. Northern or border states that witnessed important battles included Missouri, Pennsylvania, and Kentucky, despite the state's official declaration of neutrality.

The Union Forces

The country was woefully unprepared for war. That spring, the U.S. military consisted of between 16,000 and 17,000 men, most of them stationed out West in Indian country. President Lincoln immediately called for 75,000 militiamen for 90-day enlistments to serve as an expanded American fighting force.

Any military strategy implemented by the Union Army, whether long-range or short, faced extreme challenges. The federal army was limited and out of date. At the opening of the war, the army had no general staff and no organized mobilization plan. Few Union officers even had accurate maps of the South—Union commander General Henry Halleck, stationed in the West, was forced to buy maps in a St. Louis bookstore. Many of the army's high-level commanders were old. Of the army's eight bureau heads, seven had been in service since the War of 1812, and the two most experienced officers were over the age of 70.

Most of the weapons stored in government arsenals were old muskets, whose smoothbore barrels fired their bullets with wild inaccuracy. Many of these old guns were flintlocks, a completely outdated weapon by 1860. There were not enough cannons or general artillery for the coming war effort immediately available either. But, within a matter of weeks of the opening of the conflict, the army began ordering nearly everything it might need for a war.

The president also ordered a naval blockade of the Confederate coast. But it was a paper order only. The U.S. Navy was woeful. That spring the navy had only 42 commissioned ships in the water, and most of them were patrolling thousands of miles from American waters. Many of them were outdated, wooden-hulled ships using canvas sails. Only 12 or so were fit for combat. One advantage the navy did have was that few naval personnel left their commands and joined the Confederacy. Also, the North had a large number of civilian-owned merchant ships that could be purchased and refitted for naval duty. By the end of 1861 the federal navy had expanded to 260 warships, with 100 additional vessels under construction, including a handful of newly designed ships made of iron, the famous ironclads of the Civil War era.

The Secession of Virginia

President Davis ordered up 100,000 Southern volunteers, calling on them to fight to secure the South's independence. Four more states seceded after the attack on Fort Sumter—Virginia (April 17), Arkansas (May 6), Tennessee (May 7), and North Carolina (May 20). The remaining four slave states—Missouri, Delaware, Maryland, and Kentucky—remained in the Union, even as Kentucky declared its neutrality. Over the next two years, the western portion of Virginia chose to secede from the remainder of the state, becoming West Virginia, which was admitted into the Union on June 19, 1863.

The secession of Virginia had two immediate results. The capital of the Confederacy was moved to Richmond, Virginia, and a longtime veteran of the U.S. Army, Virginian Robert E. Lee, resigned his commission and joined the Confederate Army. This was considered a major loss for the federal government at the time, since Lee had been approached to command the U.S. Army in the coming war. Lee believed in the Union, did not support secession, and was even opposed to the institution of slavery. But once Virginia seceded, his decision followed. With words noted by historian Charles P. Roland, Lee stated: "I cannot raise my hand against my birthplace, my home, my children."

With Virginia's secession, Confederate troops were soon placed along the state's northern border, the Potomac River.

Some were garrisoned opposite Washington, D.C., which was soon filled with Union volunteers and regular forces. During the early weeks of the war, troops were housed in both the Senate and House chambers until tent camps could be established to accommodate the thousands who were arriving daily.

When Congress took up a special session on July 4, 1861, its members were prepared to support President Lincoln and the federal military. Republican Thaddeus Stevens, the Chairman of the House Ways and Means Committee, provided superb leadership. Within their first five days of meeting, the House approved a bill allowing Secretary of the Treasury, Salmon P. Chase, to borrow $250 million—a gigantic sum of money in that day—over the following 12 months to pay for the war effort. Over the next two months Congress passed a total of 62 bills related to the war. Such productivity was possible, in part, due to the absence of Southerners in the House and Senate.

THE LEDGER OF WAR

Even with the decision of the "border states" to remain in the Union, those supporting the Confederacy were confident. They knew that they only had to fight a defensive war, just as their colonial ancestors had fought against the British, and they were keenly aware of the advantages they held. Many of those who joined the Confederate Army were men of the outdoors, who knew how to shoot and ride. They would be fighting on familiar ground to protect their homes and families, as well as their overall causes. They believed that the average Confederate soldier would be able to outfight his Yankee counterpart, since such men would include factory workers, urbanites, and pasty-faced office clerks. The Confederates also knew they had great military leaders who had joined their cause, fellow Southerners who were among the best graduates of West Point, including Albert Sidney Johnston, Thomas Jackson, P.G.T. Beauregard, and, of course, Robert E. Lee.

Nevertheless, the South also entered the war with a laundry list of limitations, even liabilities. They would always

Confederate volunteers in Richmond, Virginia, pose for a photographer before the Battle of First Bull Run in 1861.

lack manpower irrespective of how successful they might be. The total population of the Confederate states was only 9 million people, and at least 3.5 million of them were slaves, who could not be relied on for military service. This compared to 22 million people in the North. Southerners also lacked the material capacity to fight a prolonged war. Throughout the four-year conflict, Confederate troops often went without food, uniforms, any supplies, medical care, ammunition, and even pay.

Four out of every five of America's factories were located in the North. In fact, the value of the goods manufactured in Northern factories was more than 11 times that of Southern industry ($1.73 billion compared to $155 million). Two out of every three miles of railroad track was Northern, and many Southern lines did not connect to one another. The North was home to 65 percent of the nation's farmland, and boasted most of the nation's banks, shipping, insurance companies, stock market investment, and mineral wealth. Federal armies would generally go into the field well equipped, well fed, and well armed.

During the war, the South captured more cannon than the Confederacy produced in its own foundries, even though Richmond was home to the largest gun foundry in the United States, the Tredegar Iron Works, which prior to the war had produced cannon for the U.S. Army. Tredegar turned out the majority of the 3,000 cannon the Confederacy manufactured.

Incorrect Policies

The South also suffered throughout the conflict from its own form of government. The Rebels had organized around a confederacy, which recognized the states as sovereign, as state rights had always been a political calling card of Southerners. This meant the South was to fight a revolution based on a conservative cause. The Confederate Constitution emphasized local rights, which put strains on how Davis and his government could conduct business throughout the war. He might request troops from a given state, but if that state's governor refused to cooperate, there was little the Rebel government could do.

Early in the war Southerners also misplaced their hopes on the single commodity that had supported slavery throughout the nineteenth century to date—cotton. They believed they could rely on cotton's marketability to help finance the war effort. Confederate officials thought, by denying cotton sales to both England and France, that one or the other foreign power would be drawn to support the Rebel cause as a means of getting Southern cotton. But the strategy did not pan out. At the beginning of the war, European warehouses were stuffed with surplus cotton, plus other sources were available, such as Egypt and India. With no significant market, plus an eventual Union naval blockade, the South's cotton made no significant contribution to the Confederate cause. These were all important factors that would help determine the ultimate outcome of the war between the states.

Northern Strategies

The Federals relied primarily on two strategies. The army's commanding general, 74-year-old Winfield Scott, was a veteran of American wars dating back to the War of 1812. Due to his age, he did not remain in command of the army for long after the war opened. Weighing in at more than 300 pounds (136 kilograms), he was too heavy to even mount a horse. However, Scott established the overall, long-term strategy for the Union, one he referred to as his "Anaconda Plan." This called for a close blockade of the Confederate coast, just as Lincoln had called for, to contain the South, plus an amphibious campaign along the Mississippi River to take control of the vast interior waterway, which would allow Federal forces to cut off the western Rebel states, including Louisiana, Arkansas, and Texas. Meanwhile, several Union armies were to move about inland and progressively take control of vital locations across the South. Scott's plan called for Union military and naval forces to squeeze the Confederacy into submission, just as an anaconda constricts around its victims.

The Anaconda Plan could not be implemented immediately, however, and was based on the expectation that the war would stretch out for several years. Another, short-range plan was also implemented, usually called the "On to Richmond" strategy. This plan called for a straight-on military advance from bases in and around Washington, D.C. south to the Confederate capital of Richmond. The strategy assumed that, if federal forces could capture the Rebel seat of government, including President Davis and the Confederate Congress, the war would be brought to an immediate conclusion and Union victory. Throughout the war, various Union generals made their own attempts to march on Richmond, without success, until General Ulysses Grant finally succeeded at the end of the four-year conflict. As for the Anaconda Plan, it was fully implemented after several years of fighting.

THE BATTLE OF BULL RUN

General Scott may have had a long-range plan that he expected to put in operation, but he immediately faced pressure from politicians and the press to launch an "On to Richmond" offensive. He tried to postpone an immediate advance, telling his critics that those volunteers who had only recently enlisted needed more time to train and prepare for war before being sent into battle. But Lincoln bowed to the pressure and instructed Scott to send troops across the

Potomac into Virginia. Besides, the federal army needed to make some overt move soon, as the 90-day enlistments of the earliest volunteers were about to expire.

Thirty-five thousand Union forces marched onto southern soil toward Richmond under the command of Brigadier General Irvin McDowell, who was regular army. In front of him was a Confederate force of 20,000 men, commanded by General P.G.T. Beauregard, who had ordered the firing on Fort Sumter three months earlier. As McDowell moved his men, he was aware of an additional 12,000 Confederate troops, under the command of General Joseph Johnston, who were encamped just 50 miles (80 km) to the west in the Shenandoah Valley. To keep those forces busy, McDowell sent Major General Robert Patterson to engage them. But Johnston and his men outmaneuvered Patterson, distracting him by leaving behind a handful of Rebel troops, and then hotfooted it over to the rail junction near where Beauregard was encamped—Manassas.

"Stonewall" Jackson Holds Firm

As McDowell came near to Beauregard's forces, the Union general's plan was to strike hard against the Southern army's left flank. But the Confederate Creole commander had plans of his own, which involved his intention to take up the battle by attacking McDowell's left flank, on the opposite end of the line. After both armies completed their efforts to place themselves in the best position for a fight, the battle began on Sunday, July 21. It was a hot summer day, yet people streamed out of Washington, D.C., only 30 or so miles (50 km) to the northeast, to watch their gallant boys in blue trounce the Rebels and end the war by sundown. Government officials, including members of Congress, rode out to the site of the impending fight with their wives, who had packed picnic baskets.

A group of Union soldiers turn from their defeat at the First Battle of Bull Run on July 21, 1861. As they left the battlefield, they threw away their blankets, knapsacks, canteens, and even muskets. Soon after, the Confederate troops came to collect the equipment and added it to its stock.

That morning, McDowell put his plan into action, striking powerfully against the Confederate line, as his men concentrated on the enemy's left. Rebel troops began to fold up, seemingly overwhelmed by superior numbers. For a moment, it appeared the battle would be short and victory certain for the Union.

But even as several portions of the Southern line retreated in a panic, the Rebel center held fast, led by a Virginia brigade commanded by an eccentric West Point graduate and instructor at Virginia Military Institute, Thomas Jackson. As Southern resistance held its ground around Jackson, the otherwise panicking Rebels gained a rallying point. Historian Geoffrey Ward notes how one wounded Southern general, Bernard Bee, according to legend, shouted to his South Carolina troops: "Look! There is Jackson standing like a stone wall! Rally behind the Virginians!" Although Bee died soon after, his men heeded his call, took up positions around Jackson and rallied as instructed. That day, Thomas Jackson became immortalized as "Stonewall" Jackson.

A Confederate Victory

It was a turning point in the battle. Over the next few hours, the fight seesawed back and forth as first one side, then the other, gained advantage. It was a dreadful day for an engagement, as the weather was stifling hot, causing some men to fall from heat exhaustion. Then, as the battle raged, the Confederates received much needed reinforcements. Fresh troops reached the field under Joe Johnston's command, along with cavalry forces under Colonel Jubal A. Early. Other Rebel soldiers reached the Manassas battlefield by train.

For 14 hours, thousands of soldiers, most of them new to fighting, had engaged in an inconclusive battle, with no food or even water. But with their reinforcements, the Confederates now gained the upper hand and were able to push until the Federal line wavered, then collapsed in panicked confusion. Jackson then rallied his men, ordering them to shout loudly in the face of the retreating Federals. Their shouts gave birth to what became known as the "Rebel Yell."

Suddenly those civilians who had come out to witness the battle found themselves in harm's way. With only one road leading back to Washington, the dusty lane became a jumbled tangle of carriages, men and women in their Sunday dress, and worn-out soldiers anxious to remove themselves from the field of fighting. The retreat became known later as "The Great Skedaddle," and some Union troops did not stop running until the following Monday morning, when they reached Washington. The battle—known to Northerners as Bull Run and to Southerners as Manassas—was the first significant engagement of the war since Fort Sumter.

It was a day of Confederate victory, yet the casualties were sobering. Union losses amounted to 2,896 men compared to 1,982 Confederate casualties. (A casualty of war includes those killed, wounded, captured, or missing.) No previous battle in American history had ever produced a casualty rate as high. Yet compared to later battles, the losses of Bull Run would seem modest. Both sides realized that the war would not be over soon, and that both North and South could expect an extended conflict.

4

The War in the West, 1861–1862

The Union's loss on the Bull Run battlefield proved embarrassing to Northerners, both soldier and civilian alike. In less than a week Lincoln made significant changes in his commanders. He replaced the 74-year-old Winfield Scott with another general less than half Scott's age. Thirty-four-year-old George B. McClellan, a West Point graduate who finished second in his class, had already distinguished himself in a small engagement in western Virginia. In early June, having marched his men from Ohio, McClellan met a small Confederate force, surprising them in the midst of a rainy downpour at Philippi, Virginia. Although the fight was little more than a skirmish, McClellan had succeeded in capturing hundreds of Confederate troops, while hundreds more retreated in what Northerners later referred to as the "Philippi Races."

The fight had not amounted to much, but it was a much-needed win for the North, so McClellan had received lots of press. It was also followed up by other local victories for the young Ohioian. McClellan's efforts in western Virginia that spring were important because they allowed the Union to hold onto the region. Ultimately, 25,000 western Virginians would fight for the North, compared to 15,000 who sided with the Confederacy.

Initially, General McClellan—a short, compact man of whom it was said had the ability to lift a 250-lb (115-kg) man over his head—seemed an appropriate pick to command the Union forces. He was an excellent organizer, who brought discipline to the green volunteers who joined the Northern army. He banned drunkenness, removed unqualified officers, and oversaw the layout of tidy tent cities all around Washington. He spent months, nearly a year, preparing his men to engage the enemy. But he took no overt action against the Rebels in Virginia.

There was little action in the eastern theater for the remainder of 1861. The only standout incident was a skirmish at Ball's Bluff, outside Washington, on October 21. The fight occurred when a small unit of Union troops was sent across the Potomac River to test the strength of Confederate positions. Two hundred and twenty-three Federal soldiers were killed, some as they tried to swim back across the Potomac to safety.

By this time McClellan's army numbered more than 120,000 men, yet he did not march against the Confederates. As criticism of the egotistical commander grew, he only became more hostile, writing a letter to his wife, as noted by historian Geoffrey Ward, in which he complained: "I am here in a terrible place. The enemy have three or four times my force; the president, the old general [Winfield Scott], cannot or will not see the true state of affairs... I am thwarted and deceived... at every turn." Despite McClellan's belief, his army vastly outnumbered the Confederates across the river.

FIGHTING OUT WEST

While McClellan refused to budge from his headquarters in Washington, fighting did take place in the developing western theater of the war. In August 1861 there was action in Missouri at Wilson's Creek outside Springfield, a fight the Confederates won, causing Missouri to split in half between those who supported the North and those loyal to the South. Although this important border state never seceded from the Union, it remained divided throughout the war. Ultimately, more Missourians fought for the Union (80,000) than joined the ranks of the Confederacy (30,000). In addition, another 3,000 Missourians sided with irregular forces, guerrillas who generally harassed through hit-and-run tactics.

Elsewhere in Missouri General John C. Fremont (the 1856 Republican candidate for president), who was in command of the West, placed a little-known brigadier general from Illinois in command of Union forces in that state. Ulysses S. Grant had attended West Point, where he had not generally excelled as a student. He later fought in the Mexican War. After various postings in the Far West during the 1850s, he resigned his commission and returned to civilian life, where he and his family struggled to make ends meet. With the opening of the war, Grant had returned to military service.

Grant and his forces were sent into Kentucky in September 1861 to secure the state for the Union. After engaging Rebels in Missouri, he marched to Paducah, Kentucky, where he captured the outlets of both the Tennessee and Cumberland Rivers—two major interior rivers that cut across the South and flow into the Ohio River. By early February, Grant began to advance on two forts, Fort Henry and Fort Donelson. These two Confederate strongholds, one on the Tennessee River, the other on the Cumberland, were blocking Union access up those major streams. Grant easily captured Fort Henry on February 6, then followed up his victory

The Trent Incident

During the fall of 1861, as President Lincoln tried to prod General McClellan into action, he also dealt with another difficult situation. On November 8 a U.S. Navy vessel, the *U.S.S. San Jacinto,* intercepted a British mail ship, the *Trent,* en route from Havana, Cuba, to the Virgin Islands. Two Confederate diplomats—John Slidell from Louisiana and James Mason of Virginia—bound for Paris and London were taken prisoner by the commander of the U.S. ship, Captain Charles Wilkes. Slidell had served in Congress during the 1840s and had negotiated with the Mexican government during the Mexican–American War. His brothers-in-law included the Southern General P.G.T. Beauregard and American Naval Commodore Matthew Perry.

The two Southerners were on a diplomatic mission at the time of their capture. The South was seeking support for its war efforts from the British and French governments. If either European power had entered the war, either militarily or with economic aid, the South would have gained significantly from their involvement. Realizing the importance of his two captives, Captain Wilkes took them to Boston and placed them in a Union prison. The Northern press learned of the *Trent* Incident, and touted Wilkes as a hero. Congress even struck a special medal to honor him.

However, the British government was outraged. A U.S. Navy vessel had forcefully detained a British ship. For a time there was some talk in London of Britain going to war with the Union over the incident. The Lincoln administration soon intervened. Secretary of State William Seward declared that the American war vessel had taken illegal steps by imprisoning the two Confederate diplomats and not bringing the case before an admiralty court. Although the British Prime Minister, Viscount Palmerston, delivered an ultimatum to the president, demanding an apology, Lincoln merely released Mason and Slidell by the end of December. The president never formally apologized for the Navy's actions. Mason and Slidell resumed their voyage to England but failed in their mission.

10 days later with the capture of Fort Donelson. There, he was forced to lay down a siege of the Confederate fort. The fort commander, General Simon B. Buckner, surrendered on February 16 and delivered 15,000 prisoners to the Union Army. When Buckner and Grant met one another in the field, it was a reunion of sorts, as the two men had been roommates at West Point.

Grant's reputation across the North began to spread. After the success of this siege, Grant told reporters that he was a smoker (of pipes), and adoring Northerners began sending the Union commander boxes, even barrels of cigars. At that point Grant took up a 20-cigars-a-day habit.

THE BATTLE OF SHILOH

From Fort Donelson, Grant moved his army of 42,000 men south into Tennessee, headed for Corinth, Mississippi, where he planned to take control of the local rail line. By March he had reached the western banks of the Tennessee River, near a settlement called Pittsburg Landing. A Confederate force of about 50,000 men, under the command of General Albert Sidney Johnston, was encamped just 20 miles (32 km) away at Corinth. They were aware of Grant's position, although Grant was unaware of how close the Rebels were to him. Johnston's number two in the field was General P.G.T. Beauregard.

Johnston was a tough and seasoned military man. He had served in the U.S. Army for decades prior to the war and Robert E. Lee, who later became the South's greatest general of the war, had served under him in Texas during the 1850s. Johnston did not intend to wait for Grant to attack him. Instead, he surprised Grant on the morning of April 6, a Sunday. The Rebels routed the Federals that day, driving them back to the Tennessee River with no means of escape. Johnston was mortally wounded on the field, as a Yankee

The recapture of artillery by Union forces during the battle of Shiloh, Tennessee, April 6–7, 1862. Much of the battle was between small units of troops fighting at point-blank range in the mud of the banks of the Tennessee River.

bullet severed his femoral artery. During the Union retreat, General Beauregard occupied the tent of one of Grant's chief generals, William Tecumseh Sherman.

However, Grant was reinforced that night with 25,000 fresh troops under the command of General Don Carlos Buell, who arrived by steamboats. The second day of fighting at Pittsburg Landing reversed the equation, as exhausted Confederates engaged Buell's newly arrived men. Beauregard's weary 30,000 could not match the larger Union force of more than 50,000, and the Confederates fell back. Later that afternoon Beauregard retreated back to Corinth.

Once again, Ulysses S. Grant found his name in the Northern papers. The battle at Pittsburgh Landing, also called the battle of Shiloh after a small local Methodist church, was a singular victory for the North, even though it was a fight that Grant had nearly lost. More than 100,000 men had fought along the banks of the Tennessee River, and one out of every four became a casualty. Nearly 3,500 men were killed in those two days of fighting, more than had fallen in all the battles of the American Revolution, the War of 1812, and the Mexican–American War combined. But the victory was savored by the Union. Grant's win at Shiloh that spring was crucial for the North to control western Tennessee and that portion of the Mississippi River.

THE WAR ON WATER

That same spring Union forces were busy along other stretches of the Mississippi River. The long-term Union strategy, based on the "Anaconda Plan," had always set a priority on Union occupation of the great Midwestern River that flowed through New Orleans into the Gulf of Mexico.

Just two days before the opening shots were fired at Shiloh, a Union gunboat, the *Carondelet,* ran the river past Island No. 10, a Confederate stronghold on the Mississippi, located near the Missouri boot heel. With a Union vessel south of the island, local Rebel shore batteries had no choice but to surrender. Island No. 10 fell into Union hands on April 8, 1862. The Confederate surrender was handed to Union General John Pope, which led to Pope's receiving a promotion, and even command of the Union forces in the eastern theater by mid-summer. At the mouth of the river, additional Union forces captured New Orleans by the end of the month. By early June, Federals had captured Memphis. Slowly, but with deliberate action, the Union was gaining control of the Mississippi River.

In other naval action, Southern President Jefferson Davis had announced during the opening days of the war that any ship wanting to raid Northern merchant vessels should do so. As a result, hundreds of Union ships were stopped on the high seas and seized by privateers sympathetic to the South. President Lincoln responded by announcing that any privateers captured by the U.S. Navy would be hanged. When Davis reacted by threatening to execute a Union prisoner for every Southern privateer hanged, Lincoln backed down, ordering privateers to be held as prisoners of war. Nevertheless, Southern privateers roamed the American coastline during the first two years of the war, capturing dozens of merchant ships. By that time, the Confederate navy had enough ships to carry out such raids on its own. All told, more than 250 Northern vessels were destroyed by Southern raiders during the war.

New Naval Technologies

Perhaps the most unique aspect of the naval fighting that occurred during the Civil War centered on the new technologies used by both sides. Southerners pioneered floating mines, called torpedoes at the time, which destroyed nearly four dozen Union warships before the war's end. The South is also credited with building the first military submarine, the *H.C. Hunley*. It was only used once during the war. On the night of February 17, 1864, the eight-man crew of the cigar-shaped iron submersible torpedoed a Union blockade vessel off the coast of Charleston Harbor. The *Hunley* never returned from the attack, lost at sea, along with its crew. The wreck of the *Hunley* was rediscovered on the floor of the harbor in 2000 and has been recovered for museum display.

One of the most innovative technologies of the war was the development of an entirely new kind of surface vessel—the ironclad. In an age when ships were wooden sailing vessels, the ironclads redefined the art of naval warfare. The first was Southern made. In 1861, as the North abandoned the naval yard at Norfolk, Virginia, they scuttled a wooden steam frigate, the *Merrimack,* to keep it out of the hands of the Rebels. Confederates later raised the sunken ship and bolted iron plates over its hull, creating a new kind of vessel, one capable of withstanding a naval cannon barrage. Earlier wooden sailing ships designed for warfare had sometimes had portions of their hulls sheathed in copper, both for defense and to protect the wood from shipworms, but never the entire ship. Southerners rechristened their redesigned dreadnought the *CSS Virginia.*

The North did not intend to be outdone at sea, however. The first Union ironclad, though, was not constructed from an existing wooden ship. It was invented from the ground up by a Swedish immigrant, John Ericsson, who had done work for the U.S. Navy before the war. Working out of New York City, Ericsson designed an odd-looking craft that was made entirely of iron and sat low and flat in the water. The most innovative feature was its revolving iron turret, which allowed its two guns to fire in any direction. Ericsson built his ship, the *Monitor,* in just four months, since the *Virginia* was already in existence. There were plenty of problems, including the ventilation system, which failed during tests, causing the crew to pass out. But the new fighting ship was launched into the cold waters of New York's East River on January 30, 1862.

Battle of the Ironclads

The launch was not a day too soon. As the *Monitor* steamed south to Virginia, the *Virginia* was planning an attack against several Union Naval vessels tied up at Hampton Roads. On March 8 the ironclad Rebel vessel sank the 50-gun U.S. frigate, *Cumberland.* The *Virginia* then fired red-hot cannon balls at another Union warship, the *Congress,* setting it on fire. Low tides kept the ironclad from attacking a third Yankee ship, the *Minnesota,* and the *Virginia* withdrew, its crew intending to return the following morning to finish her off.

When the Rebel ship did steam toward the helpless wooden ship at 7 A.M. on March 9, its crew saw a strange looking craft in position. It was the *Monitor.* What unfolded was one of the most unique sea battles in history. For the first time ever, two ironclad ships attacked one another, in a duel that lasted for four hours. During much of the fight, the two ships fired on each other at close range, sitting nearly hull to hull in the water. Although the *Virginia* sported ten deadly guns to the *Monitor's* two, the Union ship did not have to maneuver into position to fire, thanks to its revolving turret. Ericsson's vessel was also quicker. And it made a smaller target, since it was half the length of the *Virginia* and sat so low in the water. Although both crews landed direct hits on their enemy vessel, the cannonballs only caused limited damage. Finally, after each had received approximately two dozen direct hits, the battle was broken off, and the *Virginia* withdrew. It would be the last time the two ironclads would engage one another. Later, the Rebels scuttled the *Virginia* to keep it out of Union hands (just as the Federals had done

The naval engagement between the Union *Monitor* and the Confederate *Virginia* on March 9, 1862. The two ironclads fought for some hours at close range but neither side seemed to gain an advantage.

with the *Merrimack* the previous year). As for the *Monitor,* it later floundered in a storm off the coast of North Carolina. But naval warfare would never again be the same.

ACTION IN CONGRESS

The war had been underway for a year by the spring of 1862 and the costs of the conflict had already reached staggering proportions. The war was costing the federal government $2 million a day, an enormous sum at that time. Congress passed a bill on February 6, authorizing the issuing of "greenbacks," paper money to be used as legal tender to pay for war purchases and other financing. Congress also passed, on April 16, a bill outlawing slavery in the nation's capital. Those who owned slaves there could either leave or be compensated. This move constituted one of the first steps in the ultimate legislating of slavery out of existence. Lincoln was reluctant to sign the bill, however. At that time, the president continued to balk at making slavery a significant issue of the war, as he was still concerned about the border states leaving the Union.

Despite the war, Congress busied itself with additional important legislation. In May 1862 the Homestead Act was passed, which provided 160 acres (65 hectares) of federally owned land out West to anyone who would move there and occupy the land for five years. Tens of thousands of Americans took the opportunity within the new act's first two years, claiming over 3 million acres (1 million ha) of land. Then, in June, Congress passed the Morrill Land Grant College Act, which provided monies from the sale of 30,000 acres (12,000 ha) of public land to each member of Congress. This was to be used to finance the establishment of public educational institutions within each state, dedicated to teaching the agricultural and mechanical arts. Land grant colleges sprang up across the country over the next few decades.

Two other important acts were passed by Congress during the war. The Internal Revenue Act of 1862 placed a tax on a long list of items. While the scope of the act itself did not last until the end of the war, the act created the Bureau of Internal Revenue, which did. The second significant act was the Pacific Railroad Act of 1862. For years, Congress had debated on a viable railroad route across the West, but sectional differences had always made an agreement impossible. With the South now out of the picture, Congress passed the act. It provided monies and land for the building of the first transcontinental rail line across the country, the route based between Omaha, Nebraska, and Sacramento, California.

5

The Summer of War, 1862

A week following the epic sea battle between the two ironclads, *Monitor* and *Virginia*, George McClellan finally took his first offensive steps against the Rebels. For most of a year, he had organized and drilled his immense army on the outskirts of Washington. Through those endless months, his lack of will to move his army against the enemy had frustrated President Lincoln, his cabinet, and the War Department.

THE PENINSULA CAMPAIGN

Finally, however, McClellan was on the march. McClellan believed he had developed an ironclad plan of his own with which to meet his enemy. Rather than engage in an overland campaign covering the 100 miles (160 km) between Washington and Richmond, the resourceful general had organized a variation on the "On to Richmond" strategy. He would transport his army down the Potomac to Chesapeake Bay, and land them on the Virginia Peninsula lying east of

Richmond, between the York and the James Rivers. His army included 120,00 men; 15,000 horses and mules; more than 1,100 wagons; 44 artillery batteries; 74 ambulance wagons; and a massive collection of equipment—including everything from collapsible pontoon bridges to tents to telegraph wire. From the Virginia Peninsula, he intended to move his men toward Richmond, with the two rivers protecting his

A 12-lb (5.3-kg) howitzer captured from the Rebels by Union forces led by Major Daniel Butterfield's Brigade near Hanover Court House, Virginia, on May 27, 1862. A howitzer is a gun with a short barrel that is used as a long-range mortar.

flanks from enemy attack. Lincoln and his Secretary of War, Edwin Stanton, had been tepid on the plan, but had signed off on it, ready for McClellan to move against the Rebels. The plan was thoughtful and well organized. Its primary problem proved to be McClellan himself.

When McClellan finally moved his men toward Virginia soil by ship, President Davis and his chief military officer, General Robert E. Lee, were concerned that McClellan's army was not the only Federal force in Virginia capable of menacing Richmond. When McClellan had organized his force, Lincoln had ordered him to leave 40,000 men behind to protect Washington, D.C. from Confederate attack. So the Southern leaders sent General Stonewall Jackson and his men into Northern Virginia to keep those Union forces not directly marching with McClellan from causing any problems. This then provoked Northern fears that Jackson's forces would move against the Union capital if it were not properly defended.

Any concern over Jackson was well founded. Jackson had already gained a fierce reputation as a no-nonsense Confederate commander who drove his men hard and won battles. He was an eccentric and a hypochondriac, who did not eat pepper because he believed it made his left leg ache and who always sat bolt upright, thinking that slouching caused his internal organs to fall out of balance. He was also a highly religious individual—a Confederate commander with a Joshua complex, who told his men they marched as the arm of the Lord. Jackson's men were not fond of him, but they followed him wherever he ordered them.

Even as McClellan and his immense force sailed toward Fortress Monroe at Hampton on the Virginia Peninsula in March, Jackson took 20,000 men into the Shenandoah Valley in central Virginia, which lay just west of the Blue Ridge of the Appalachian chain. The Valley provided Jackson with cover, shielding his movements. By sliding his army up and down the Valley—he marched his "foot cavalry" as many as 40 miles (64 km) a day—Jackson managed to keep three separate Union armies, a total of 75,000 blue-clad enemy troops, off balance and away from Richmond for nearly two months. Only once during his Valley Campaign did Jackson lose a fight, the one at Kernstown on March 23. On June 8 he won a late battle against General Fremont's army at Cross Keys, then another at Port Republic on June 9. Then he ordered his men to rush south to join Lee's Army of Northern Virginia for the battles against McClellan.

THE BATTLE OF FAIR OAKS

As for McClellan, even after landing his forces on the Peninsula, the federal commander took his time, moving timidly forward, certain that he was outnumbered by the enemy. In fact, he had vastly superior numbers himself. By early April 1862, with the war a year old, Lincoln was desperate for McClellan to do something, anything, to give the appearance that he intended to use his army in a forceful campaign. On April 9 the president sent a note to McClellan, as historian Allen Weinstein notes:

> *Once more, let me tell you, it is indispensable to you that you strike a blow.... The country will not fail to note—is now noting—that the present hesitation to move upon an intrenched enemy is but the story of Manassas repeated.*

Still McClellan crept slowly along, taking two months to reach Yorktown on the peninsula. Occupying the town where the British General Cornwallis had surrendered to Washington during the Revolutionary War, the Union commander moved forces to within 6 miles (10 km) of Richmond. Federal soldiers could see church spires in the distance and hear the bells in those towers ringing. But McClellan's delaying had provided time for the Rebels to mass in larger numbers east of the Confederate capital, where they engaged the Union Army on May 31–June 1 in the Battle of Seven Pines, also remembered as Fair Oaks.

An Enforced Change of Command

The Confederate commander, General Joseph Johnston, took advantage of the fact that McClellan's army was divided by the Chickahominy River. Johnston sent two Rebel corps along the south banks of the river, intending to drive them hard against the enemy. But a lack of communication, along with an uncharacteristically poor showing by General Stonewall Jackson, caused the battle to descend into little more than a draw. The fighting had been intense, however, and Johnston was severely wounded.

This significant casualty would cause Confederate president Jefferson Davis, who rode out of Richmond to watch the battle unfold, to replace Johnston with Robert E. Lee. General Lee would remain the commander of the Army of Northern Virginia for the rest of the war. According to historian Earle Rice, when Johnston, lying wounded in a hospital in Richmond, received word of Lee's new command, he told a friend: "The shot that struck me down is the best that has been fired for the Southern cause yet, for I possess in no degree the confidence of our government, and now they have in place one who does."

THE SEVEN DAYS BATTLES

The Battle of Fair Oaks helped set the stage for a series of battles nearly three weeks later between Lee and McClellan that became known as the Seven Days. But before Lee engaged the Federals as the Army of Northern Virginia's new commander, he sent his best cavalry commander, J.E.B. Stuart, with 1,200 mounted troopers on a reconnaissance mission. Through three days, Stuart and his men rode 150 miles (240 km) in a circle around McClellan's army, burning Yankee tent encampments, taking prisoners, and stealing 300 horses and mules. When Stuart reported back, Lee had the information he needed. He also had with him the best of the Confederate officer corps, including the likes of Stonewall Jackson, James Longstreet, Ambrose P. Hill, and D. H. Hill.

Even though his men were outnumbered on the battlefield, Lee engaged McClellan day after day for a solid week. The fight began on June 25 at Oak Grove, then Mechanicsville, or Beaver Dam Creek, which resulted in a hasty Union retreat, on June 26, followed by Gaines's Mill on June 27, then Savage's Station on June 29, White Oak Swamp and Frayser's Farm, or Glendale, on June 30, with the week ending at Malvern Hill on July 1.

Throughout these battles, the advantage shifted from one side to the other. During the Seven Days, as Lee pushed hard against McClellan, some of the Union general's subordinate officers suggested that he should advance directly on Richmond, believing that Lee had left only a small force to defend the city. While they were correct, McClellan would have none of it. At Malvern Hill McClellan accomplished a clear win over Lee, with the Rebels sustaining heavy casualties during a series of uphill frontal attacks. The fighting was intense. Historian Ward recalls the words of a Union colonel after the battle:

> *Our ears had been filled with agonizing cries from thousands before the fog was lifted, but now our eyes saw [that] five thousand dead or wounded men were on the ground. A third of them were dead or dying, but enough of them were alive and moving to give the field a singular crawling effect.*

Yet after the battle was over, the Union commander could not even recognize the victory. He ordered a general retreat back to the relative safety of the James River.

Although Union forces won as many battles during the Seven Days as Lee did, McClellan nevertheless continued to believe that his army was outnumbered. He did not follow

Wounded troops are treated at a field hospital at Savage's Station, Virginia, after the battle of June 27, 1862—the fourth of the Seven Days Battles. For every man killed in battle during the U.S. Civil War, two died of poor sanitation, lack of food and water, or mosquito-borne infections.

up his Malvern Hill victory, but ordered Federal defenses abandoned. A month later his men were encamped at Harrison's Landing and the long-planned Peninsula Campaign was over.

The Seven Days week of fighting resulted in nearly 35,000 casualties (this figure includes both the wounded and those killed). This was an appalling number at that point in the war, equal to all the casualties in the western theater during the first six months of 1862, including the bloody battle of Shiloh. Northern casualties amounted to 15,800 men, compared to Lee's 20,100. The Seven Days would set the course for later battles that placed the North's Army of the Potomac against Lee's Army of Northern Virginia, engagements that required hard fighting and high casualties. In fact, throughout the war, according to historian James McPherson, "forty of the fifty highest-casualty regiments served in the Army of Northern Virginia." Lee would lead the pack as the commander with the highest casualty rate.

SECOND BULL RUN

Orders soon came down from the high command in Washington for McClellan to abandon the peninsula. He was to move his Army of the Potomac to Alexandria, Virginia, and join with Major General John Pope's force of 63,000 men, the Army of Virginia. McClellan received his orders on August 16 but, in his usual style, he moved slowly.

Lee, in the meantime, did not intend to wait around. He knew that he needed to strike before the two Federal armies came together as a single force, for Pope's and McClellan's armies combined would give the Federals a three-to-one advantage over him. And Pope was on the move. Lee ordered Stonewall Jackson to make a march around Pope's army on the Rappahannock River and attack a giant Union supply depot at Manassas Junction, near where the Bull Run battle had been fought a year earlier. Jackson made the raid on August 26, forcing Pope to turn his army. This allowed Lee to dispatch another Rebel force, under General James Longstreet, to the north to catch Pope off-guard. Longstreet

Civil War Field Tactics

Civil War soldiers on both sides were often men who were not formally trained in the arts of war. Many, in fact, became soldiers without ever having had firearms training, or experience of any kind with a gun. Yet such men were typically placed in deadly situations on the battlefield. Some of those situations were the result of outmoded battle tactics.

For centuries prior to the Civil War, armies in Europe had fought with troops lined up in formation, several columns deep, marching in unison, and firing their inaccurate weapons in volleys to maximize their killing potential. During the Revolutionary War Americans fought the same way. During the early nineteenth century the French military leader, Napoleon Bonaparte, also relied on forward infantry assaults, but made greater use of artillery to blast holes in enemy lines. The combination of the two created French armies that were killing machines.

In the Mexican–American War, U.S. Army officers relied on Napoleonic tactics, using close-order infantry assaults supported by accurate field cannons. The Americans fighting in Mexico won battles because the Mexican weapon of the day was a smoothbore musket, with a maximum range of 250 yards (230 meters) and an accuracy to only one-third of that distance.

reached Pope on August 30 and the resulting fight sent Yankee forces running from the field—the same ground as the earlier Manassas fight, thus known afterward as the Second Battle of Bull Run.

Many high-ranking officers in the Civil War—both Northern and Southern—had fought in the Mexican–American War and clung to the same basic battlefield tactics they had used successfully a generation earlier, with the exception of a new and deadly twist. The direct frontal assaults that had paid off so well for Napoleon and for U.S. forces in other conflicts now met the withering and accurate fire of rifled weapons. Cannon crews, who had previously kept 200 yds (180 m) from the enemy's front lines, out of musket range, now found themselves in harm's way, facing rifles loaded with lead bullets that included ball-shaped projectiles and cone-shaped projectiles popularly known as Minie balls.

In addition, the traditional bayonet charge—a longstanding field tactic involving double-timing infantry forces running the final 80 yds (72 m) during the 30 seconds previously required to reload most muskets—was no longer reasonable. With the invention and adoption of rifles, Napoleonic warfare from a half-century earlier had become obsolete. Rifle-wielding troops could target enemy soldiers at a greater distance; gun crews could be fired on; and the bayonet charge was little more than storming into the face of sure death. Thus, the vast majority of direct frontal assaults during the Civil War were doomed to fail, producing extremely high casualty rates. Yet the tactic was used by both sides right to the end.

Pope had moved toward Richmond with great confidence and commitment, certain he would defeat Lee's army. His famous phrase, which he repeated more than once, is recalled by historian Geoffrey Ward: "May God have mercy on Robert E. Lee, for I shall have none." Now he was crushed and humiliated. Lincoln and the War Department were so disappointed in Pope that he was removed from command in Virginia and transferred out to Minnesota to fight the Sioux, who were engaged in an uprising. Pope never again saw action in the Civil War.

As for McClellan, he was partially to blame for Pope's defeat, since he had not moved quickly to join with Pope's forces before the Battle of Second Bull Run. Historian James McPherson notes that Lincoln spoke of McClellan's failure as "unpardonable" and indicated he thought McClellan had "wanted Pope defeated." Most of Lincoln's cabinet members sent the president a letter asking for McClellan's dismissal. Secretary of the Treasury Salmon P. Chase even suggested the failed Union commander should be shot. But instead he was tapped by Lincoln once more as the commander of the Union forces in Virginia. General McDowell, who had fought and lost alongside Pope, was sent out to California for the rest of the war.

TAKING THE WAR TO MARYLAND

Through a summer of victories—the Seven Days and Second Bull Run—Lee became determined to undermine the North's will to continue the fight. He proposed to President Davis that he be allowed to march his Army of Northern Virginia into Maryland, a slave-border state, where he assumed his men would be greeted with excitement and open arms. A successful campaign on Northern soil might also convince the British to join the Confederate cause. Davis agreed, and Lee's forces crossed the Potomac by early September, singing

"Maryland, My Maryland." But Maryland residents did not greet the Rebels joyously, with many simply locking their doors and staying out of sight. One Maryland woman who did watch the Confederate Army march through the town of Frederick, as historian James F. Murfin writes, noted them as "the filthiest set of men and officers I ever saw; with clothing that . . . . had not been changed for weeks. They could be smelt all over the entire inclosure."

Lee had marched north believing that McClellan would take his time responding, as Lee informed one of his officers, Brigadier General John G. Walker:

> *Are you acquainted with General McClellan? He is an able general but a very cautious one.... His army is in a very demoralized and chaotic condition and will not be prepared for offensive operations—or he will not think it so—for three or four weeks. Before that time I hope to be on the Susquehanna [River].*

But events unfolded along a different course. On September 13 a pair of Union soldiers, stopping at an abandoned Confederate campsite in a meadow east of Frederick, found a trio of cigars wrapped within a piece of paper. A closer look revealed the paper as a copy of Lee's Special Orders No. 119, dated September 9. The paper revealed that Lee had divided his 55,000 men, and dispatched two-thirds of his forces under Stonewall Jackson to Harper's Ferry to capture the federal arsenal. The paper worked its way up the Union chain of command and landed in McClellan's hands. Suddenly, the Union commander knew of Lee's battle plans and that the Rebel general's forces were divided. McClellan, as remembered by one of his officers, John Gibbon, even stated: "Here is a paper with which if I cannot whip 'Bobbie Lee,' I will be willing to go home." A hasty move might catch Lee off-guard, but McClellan did not respond fast enough, waiting to attack Lee on September 17. Meanwhile Lee had realized his plans were exposed by September 14, when three Union corps had attacked some of Jackson's men at Harpers Ferry. He sent a courier to tell Jackson to hurry and join up with him as soon as possible.

ANTIETAM

On September 17 McClellan, after delaying for several days, sent his force of 75,000 men against Lee's army of 40,000 along Antietam Creek, located east of the Maryland town of Sharpsburg. McClellan believed he was outnumbered two-to-one.

The fight required a series of coordinated attacks that stretched in order from the Confederate left to its center to its right flank, first in a cornfield, then along a sunken road that became known as Bloody Lane, and finally around a stone bridge crossing the Antietam Creek. With the fight focusing on only a portion of the battlefield at a time, Lee was able to move troops from one hotspot to another, keeping the Union forces from utterly destroying his army. He was also aided toward the end of the day by the last of his absent troops, who arrived under General D. H. Hill's command.

It was a singularly bloody day at Antietam, with concentrations of fighting delivering death throes to thousands of soldiers on both sides. It was in fact one of the bloodiest days of the war, with 13,000 Northerners killed or wounded, along with 11,000 Rebels—that number represented a quarter of Lee's army. In all, the number of soldiers killed during the battle tallied at 2,100 Union men and 2,000 Rebels. After the battle another 2,500 died from their wounds. There were four times more casualties at Antietam than the U.S. Army suffered at the D-Day landing in France on June 6, 1944, during World War II.

Through the night of September 17–18 Lee and his men braced for a second day of fighting. With the Potomac River behind them, the Rebels could not evacuate immediately. Astonishingly, McClellan did not take up the battle for a second day, even though he had thousands of fresh troops who

Dead soldiers in front of Little Dunker Church at the battle of Antietam, also photographed by Alexander Gardner. Later it was shown that many of Gardner's war photos may have been faked: He moved bodies to give the images more impact.

had not fought on the 17th. Lee's exhausted army was able to cross over the river during the following days and escape. McClellan had lost his opportunity to ultimately crush Lee's army. As the Rebels reached Virginia soil their bands played the tune, "Carry me Back to Old Virginny."

Abraham Lincoln with General George B. McClellan (facing Lincoln) and other Union generals after the battle at Antietam, photographed by Alexander Gardner. On the extreme right is George Armstrong Custer, who would play a key role at the battle of Gettysburg the following year.

The battle of Antietam served as the first turning point of the Civil War. The Union had managed to drive the Confederate Army off of Northern soil and eliminate the threat to Maryland and even Pennsylvania, Lee's ultimate destination. Also, as McClellan had not continued the fight for a second day, Lincoln removed him from command for a second time. As a result McClellan would not play an important role for the remainder of the Civil War. And because of this Southern loss, the British never seriously considered entering the conflict as an ally of the South.

LINCOLN AND SLAVERY

Perhaps one of the most significant impacts of the battle was the issuing of Lincoln's Emancipation Proclamation. On July 22, Lincoln had decided to announce by executive order the freeing of all slaves held in Confederate territory that was not under Federal control. When he presented the idea to his cabinet they supported the important move, but it was suggested that the president might want to wait to make a public announcement until the North had won an important battle. Otherwise, the proclamation would appear as nothing more than a hollow gesture by a government that was losing the war.

In the meantime Lincoln was challenged on August 19 by the editor of the North's most influential newspaper, the *New York Tribune*. Horace Greeley wrote an editorial, titled *The Prayer of Twenty Millions,* in which he called for Lincoln to free the slaves. On July 22 Lincoln responded with an editorial of his own:

> *My paramount object in this struggle is to save the Union, and is not either to save or to destroy slavery. If I could save the Union without freeing any slaves I would do it, and if I could save it by freeing all the slaves I would do it; and if*

I could save it by freeing some and leaving others alone I would also do that. What I do about slavery and the colored race, I do because I believe it helps to save the Union; and what I forbear, I forbear because I do not believe it would help to save the Union.

With the victory at Antietam (some historians just considered the Antietam fight as a draw with no clear winner, since neither side actually surrendered), Lincoln had the green light he needed to make his announcement. The Emancipation Proclamation would represent a significant brick in the wall signaling the eventual destruction of slavery in America. However, its scope was limited. The proclamation only mentioned the freeing of slaves in regions of the South that were not under Federal control. Lincoln had worded the document that way to avoid offending the border states, who would otherwise have been expected to free their slaves. Although made public after the battle, the proclamation did not go into effect until January 1, 1863.

6 From Fredericksburg to Gettysburg

The Battle of Antietam had changed the immediate direction of the war for both sides. Lee's Army of Northern Virginia had been forced to move out of Maryland and back to Confederate soil, while the North savored a victory, even if McClellan had failed to destroy Lee's forces as originally instructed by Lincoln.

More good news reached Washington a few weeks after the Maryland battle, when Yankee and Rebel forces met at Perryville, Kentucky, on October 8, a battle which forced the Confederate Army to march back into Tennessee. At the same time Southern troops were defeated in a battle at Corinth, Mississippi, which gave the Federals control of western Tennessee. The Antietam fight combined with these western events meant the Confederacy had passed its high-water mark. The Rebels would never come as close to an ultimate victory in the Civil War as they had by the end of the summer of 1862.

MARYE'S HEIGHTS

McClellan was replaced as commander of the Army of the Potomac by Major General Ambrose E. Burnside. Once in the saddle, Burnside set about fulfilling Lincoln's wish for the army to take up the fight with Robert E. Lee's forces again. He finally engaged Lee at Marye's Heights, just west of Fredericksburg, on December 13, 1862.

Lee's men had taken up fortified positions at the crest of a slope, with many in place behind a long, stone wall, 4 feet (1.2 m) high. Before the battle reached the Heights, Burnside's main body of troops had to cross the Rappahannock, which flowed directly past the town. Efforts to lay down a pontoon bridge across the 400-foot (120-m) wide river turned nightmarish, as Federal engineers were picked off by Mississippi sharpshooters hidden in the town's waterfront warehouses. Eventually, Burnside ordered his men into the pontoons to cross the river by boat.

On the morning of December 13, Burnside ordered a direct frontal assault against Lee's 75,000 well-entrenched defenders of Marye's Heights. Although the Union men numbered 130,000, they could not match the Confederates, who occupied the high ground. Men moved forward and were cut down in rows. Each assault ended in a retreat. In all, Burnside ordered 14 charges up the hill in the face of Rebel guns. So many men were cut down that blue-clad soldiers lay on the field in stacks of two or three deep.

A brigade of Irishmen moved up the hill, getting within 25 paces of the wall, then riflemen of the 24th Georgia, nearly all of them Irishmen, too, shot them to pieces. From the top of the ridge above Marye's Heights, Robert E. Lee observed the repeated assaults by Federal forces, only to watch them fall in great numbers. At one point, he noted, as historian Douglas Southall Freeman records, "It is well that war is so terrible—we should grow too fond of it!"

A NEW YEAR OF WAR

This Federal loss represented the last significant engagement of the war for the year 1862, a year during which the Union's Army of the Potomac suffered many more losses—the Peninsula, the Seven Days, Second Bull Run, Fredericksburg, and the lost opportunities of Antietam—than victories. Yet just two weeks after the Fredericksburg loss, abolitionists across the North celebrated their greatest New Year's Day, the date on which Lincoln's Emancipation Proclamation went into effect. While the Northern war effort was generally failing, the institution of slavery was being pushed out of existence.

After Fredericksburg, both armies went into winter quarters and did not fight one another again until the spring of 1863. In the meantime, the Union's two western armies—the Army of the Cumberland in eastern Tennessee under the command of General Rosecrans, and the Army of the Tennessee under Ulysses S. Grant—remained in the field and mobile. Grant was given the objective of capturing one of the last, significant Rebel holdouts on the Mississippi River, the city of Vicksburg, Mississippi. He would spend the first six months of 1863 in this campaign. Meanwhile Rosecrans's Army of the Cumberland fought a three-day engagement that unfolded between December 30 and January 1 against a Rebel army under the leadership of General Braxton Bragg. The battle took place at Stones River (or Murfreesboro) outside Nashville, Tennessee, and involved 44,000 Union men and 35,000 Confederates.

The night before the battle began the two armies were encamped no further than 100 yards (90 meters) apart, and a lively competition between regimental bands opened up. Union musicians played "Yankee Doodle," with Southern bandmen tootling "Dixie" in response. The strains of Northern and Southern song favorites wafted across the lines until

General William S. Rosecrans on horseback rallies his troops at the battle of Stones River. The battle was tactically inconclusive, with casualties and losses amounting to more than 13,000 for the Union and 10,000 for the Confederates.

one band began playing "Home Sweet Home," only to be joined by other bands, on both sides, playing the same tune. By the time the music played out, nearly every man in both armies was singing the same song.

The battle itself was a bloody brawl of a fight, with both sides engaging to an indecisive conclusion. At one point in the battle General William S. Rosecrans was riding along on horseback as an aide riding next to him was decapitated by a cannon ball. Although Rosecrans's army was pushed back from its original position on the field, his men rallied later in the fight, taking advantage of a mistake made by Bragg, who ordered a misplaced attack on a Federal-held hill where his men were blasted apart by 45 Union cannon. Bragg's defeat came at a critical time for the North at year's end.

"FIGHTING JOE" AND CHANCELLORSVILLE

With Burnside's loss at Fredericksburg, Lincoln replaced him with yet another commander of the Army of the Potomac, Joseph Hooker. The new commander spent the winter working to build up the confidence of his men. Morale was low on the Union side at the first of the new year, and troops in Hooker's army were deserting at the rate of some 100 a day. However, Hooker was known as a tenacious general, and he drilled into his men that, come the spring of 1863, they would engage Lee's army and finally defeat him. He increased his army in size and outfitted them with the best equipment.

The crux of Hooker's strategy was based simply on his overwhelming numbers of men. By April, Hooker was ready to attack. He met Lee on ground near Fredericksburg, in a thickly wooded region that was locally known as the Wilderness. In the midst of the second-growth timber, vines, brambles, and heavy undergrowth was a little crossroads community called Chancellorsville, dominated by the Chancellor family mansion. It was here that the two armies would engage over several days, beginning on April 27.

With intelligence in hand that indicated Hooker was weakest on his right flank, Stonewall Jackson proposed that he take some men along a local 14-mile (22-km) trail through the Wilderness that would position his forces to attack Hooker's flank. Although this would badly divide Lee's army of 45,000, it might provide the Rebels with the opportunity they were looking for. Lee agreed and sent Jackson with 25,000 troops, leaving the Confederate leader with only 20,000 available forces. It was a long-odds gamble, but Lee was known for his audacity.

All through the day of May 2, Jackson and his men moved along the overgrown trail out in the Wilderness, toward the Federal right flank. The Union men in front of him were the Sixth Corps, under the command of Major General Oliver O. Howard, who had never led an entire corps in battle previously. Throughout the day, Howard had received multiple dispatches from Hooker, first calling on him to establish a defense line, then ordering him to take the offensive and pursue the enemy. Howard had not only failed to move, he had not secured his flank, which represented the furthest westward extension of Hooker's lines.

Just as the men of the Sixth, many of them German immigrant troops, were sitting down to prepare their evening meal and boil their coffee, deer and other forest animals came bounding out of the nearby woods. The Federals grabbed their guns to kill some fresh game, only to face Jackson's men emerging behind the wild animals, their clothes ragged from the thickets and brambles of the day's march. They completely surprised the Union men, and Hooker's right flank simply fell apart.

From that point until the battle had run its course, General Hooker never regained his bearings. He himself was seriously wounded on May 3, while standing on the porch of the Chancellor family house. A cannon ball hit, causing a large chunk of plaster to fall and hit Hooker on the head, knocking him unconscious. He was groggy the rest of the day, but refused to surrender command.

By May 4 the fight was over. The Battle of Chancellorsville would be marked as one of Robert E. Lee's greatest victories. The three-day battle resulted in 30,000 casualties, including 12,700 on the Confederate side and 17,200 for the Union. As for Hooker's men, they had heard over the previous months, from Hooker himself, how victory would be theirs come spring. But Hooker had failed, having fallen apart on the battlefield, and even lost his will to fight. Later, the Federal commander admitted himself, as historian Ward notes: "For once, I lost confidence in Hooker." When Lincoln received the full report on the battle and its losses, he was appalled. Historian James McPherson recalls the President's reaction: "My God! My God! What will the country say?"

THE DEATH OF STONEWALL

While Lee had accomplished one of his greatest battlefield victories of the war, he had suffered a singular loss as well. On May 2, after Jackson's men had plowed into the Union right flank, the eccentric Virginian general was accidentally shot by his own men. The incident took place after nightfall, amid the confusion of ground narrowly separating Union from Confederate front lines. Jackson and several of his subordinate officers were riding along a road when cannon fire diverted them into the woods. Rebel pickets took them for the enemy and opened fire. Jackson was wounded once in the right hand and twice in the left arm.

The wounds were severe. Hours later field surgeons removed Jackson's arm. Two days later the general was removed from the field to Guiney's Station, Virginia. He

The First Modern War

Both Union and Confederate forces relied heavily on the railroad system to move troops and weapons across the country. At the start of the war, the Confederates had one of the largest railroad systems in the world, with more than 9,000 miles (14,400 kilometers) of track. As Federal forces overran them, the Rebels destroyed many lines so they would be unusable to the enemy. Some lines were rebuilt many times by differing sides.

Supplies were delivered to and collected from railroad depots such as those at Nashville, Tennessee, and City Point, Virginia.

seemed to be recovering well through the following days. But, on May 7, he was diagnosed with pneumonia. Three days later the fiercely religious Confederate zealot died. His final words were as poignant as they were curious, words recalled by historian Peter Earle: "Let us cross over the river and rest under the shade of the trees."

Lee was devastated, as was the entire Confederacy. Prior to Jackson's death, his commander had expressed his anguish. Historian Robert Dabney notes Lee's famous words: "[Jackson] has lost his left arm, but I have lost my right." Just two months later, on the battlefield of Gettysburg, Lee would fully understand the truth of his words.

THE TURNING POINT: GETTYSBURG

With a significant victory under his belt, Lee wasted no time in requesting permission from President Davis and the Confederate leadership to launch a renewed campaign into the North. Since taking command of the Army of Northern Virginia a year earlier, Lee had repeatedly crushed the Army of the Potomac in battles that included the Seven Days, Second Bull Run, Fredericksburg, and Chancellorsville. Only Antietam stood as a partial loss on Lee's battle ledger. But that loss had driven Lee from Northern soil. Now Lee was prepared to return to the North, this time to Pennsylvania.

Under Generals Longstreet, Ambrose Hill, and Richard Ewell, Lee's men moved forward on June 3. At first Hooker intended to meet Lee's northern march with a southern one of his own—to Richmond. But that would leave Washington just as vulnerable, and Lincoln told his new commander, according to historian Geoffrey Ward: "I think Lee's army, and not Richmond, is your true objective point." Hooker turned his army of 85,000 men and began pursuing Lee. Ahead of him Lee crossed the Potomac River, moved through western Maryland, and reached Pennsylvania by mid-June.

By June 27 Lee's main column of 65,000 men had reached the Pennsylvania town of Chambersburg, where they raided the town's stores and shops, taking everything from shoes to food. In neighboring York Lee's men stole $28,000 from the local bank. They also rounded up local blacks and sent them south as escaped slaves. In the meantime Lee had lost the position of the Army of the Potomac. During these final days of June, the Federal War Department replaced Hooker as commander with Major General George G. Meade. After only a few days in command, Meade and his army stumbled into advance units of Lee's army at a Pennsylvania crossroads community called Gettysburg.

The Armies Gather

Lee learned of the advancing Union Army on June 28 from a civilian spy, a vague individual known only as Harrison, who had been an actor before the war. The Rebel commander was in no position for an immediate action, since his line stretched out for many miles. Surprised at the news, he sent some of his men into Cashtown, 9 miles (14 km) west of Gettysburg. At the same time, General Meade sent cavalry into Gettysburg to search for enemy troops.

The town of Gettysburg stood in the center of a web of 10 intersecting roads and, in the summer of 1863, was home to 2,400 citizens. Surrounding the town were well-cultivated farms and orchards, stretching across rolling hills and ridges and occasional granite outcroppings. In some ways, the terrain was designed for a Civil War battle, the region's hills and ridges perfect for establishing defensive positions for the army that might take control of the undulating landscape first.

On June 30 Southern advance units entered Gettysburg from the north, searching for shoes rumored to be stored there. Soon, the Confederates saw Union cavalry to the south, under the command of 37-year-old Brigadier General John Buford. Word was sent hurriedly to Rebel General A.P. Hill, who delivered the information to Lee. Suddenly, the time and place of the battle had been settled.

The First Day of Fighting

Over the next three days, July 1–3, both armies threw great numbers of troops into an epic battle that centered on ground just south of Gettysburg. Buford and his cavalrymen gained the high ground first and held off a larger force of Confederate infantry for several hours on the morning of July 1. At 10 A.M. the Union 1st Corps arrived, under the command of Major General John Reynolds. During the next several hours Reynolds' men held the Confederates at bay, until reinforcements arrived under Major General Oliver Howard. Reynolds was hit behind the ear and was killed during the engagement. By mid-afternoon, nearly 40,000 men were present on the field west and north of Gettysburg.

The turning point of the fight occurred around 4 P.M. Howard's troops were battling Confederates by the thousands, under the commands of General Richard Ewell (Corps II) and A.P. Hill (Corps III). The Federal forces were nearly overwhelmed, as Confederates pushed them back to take up positions on the rise of Cemetery Hill. Late in the day, Ewell broke off the fight, claiming that he did not have clear orders from General Lee. However, historian Emory Thomas notes that Lee had sent an aide to inform General Ewell "that it was necessary to press 'those people' in order to secure possession of the heights and that, if possible, he wished him to do this." Due to Ewell's reluctance to continue the fight that day, the Southern army may have lost its only possible advantage—to take the high ground from the Federals.

With the loss of the various hills and ridges south of Gettysburg during the fighting on July 1, Lee had a choice: He could remain and fight the Federals, who occupied better ground, or he could leave the scene, allow the Union Army to give chase and choose a better field of battle for his Army of Northern Virginia. But he did not leave the field. He had lost a day of fighting and failed to occupy the high ground. Lee was, nevertheless, confident. Throughout the fighting on July 1, both Lee and Meade had been rushing their forces forward to the new battlefield. Lee now had 60,000 men at his disposal, with only one unit, that under General George Pickett's command, still not present at Gettysburg, but hurrying on their way to the fight.

Men Massed for War

On the morning of July 2, Meade spread his men along the hills, forming an upside-down fishhook line that included Culp's Hill on the right, Cemetery Hill, and Cemetery Ridge, which stretched south for 2 miles (3 km). At the end of the ridge stood a pair of short peaks, known as the Round Tops. The Confederates took their places to the west, running parallel to the Union field positions.

Lee's strategy was to attack both ends of the Union line and try to dislodge the Federals from either flank. This would give the Confederates an opportunity to place artillery on high ground, with which they could blast the Yankees out of their positions on the field. Lee and Longstreet did not agree that morning, and had even disagreed the previous night, on whether the battle should unfold at all, given the superior positions of the Union side. Longstreet thought they should leave, move west, and let Meade pursue them until they found a field position that was to their advantage. He was ready for a repeat of Fredericksburg—let the Federals come to us. But Lee, sick with recurring bouts of dysentery and tired of the war in general, would not listen. According to historian Edwin Bearss, he told his right-hand general:

"The enemy is there, and I am going to attack him." Longstreet responded: "If he is there in the morning that means he wants you to attack him—a good reason for not doing so." Lee's reply was adamant, even stubborn: "I am going to whip them, or they are going to whip me." The Gettysburg battle was one that Lee fought by choice. It would prove to be one of his worst decisions of the war.

Ewell was sent against Cemetery Hill on the Union right flank, but failed to push the Federals back. Longstreet's men came closer to removing the Northern presence on the enemy's left flank, once they found an opening. That "gap" in the Union line was made accidentally when General Dan Sickles moved out of position on the left and took up the battle in a wheat field and peach orchard, ground later referred to as the "Devil's Den," due to the heat of the fight centered there.

As Confederates poured into the breach made by Sickles's misjudgment, the responsibility fell to a few hundred infantry belonging to the 20th Maine, under the command of a college professor, Colonel Joshua Lawrence Chamberlain, to defend the Union left flank. From their positions on a hill called Little Round Top, Chamberlain's men held tight, taking heavy casualties, but securing the flank. By the end of the day, Lee's two-pronged assault on the Union left and right had failed, and General Sickles had received a wound resulting in the removal of his right leg.

Pickett's Charge

July 2 ended with little gain for Lee's army. That evening, General J.E.B. Stuart arrived, too late to make a difference. He had been away from the Confederate Army for 10 days and had left Lee blind in the field. He and Lee exchanged words, and Stuart understood that he had failed his commander, allowing the fight to reach Lee before he could report back. But Lee quickly pushed aside his anger with

On July 3, 1863, at the battle of Gettysburg, both sides relied heavily on their artillery. Here, Union artillery (in the foreground) try to dominate the division of Confederate General George E. Pickett as it charges toward Cemetery Ridge (far background).

Stuart, more determined to remove the Federals from their positions along Cemetery Hill, Cemetery Ridge, and Culp's Hill than ever before.

On the evening of July 2 Lee met with his subordinate officers to plan the next day's attack. Lee was convinced the weakest portion of the Union line would be its center, since Meade had reinforced his flanks. He ordered a cannon barrage for the following morning, its purpose being to soften up the Federal center, followed by an infantry charge. But that charge would have to be made across one mile (1.5 km) of open ground, where the advancing Rebels would be extremely vulnerable. Again, Lee and Longstreet disagreed, with Longstreet insisting that no group of men could make the planned charge successfully. Lee overrode him.

On July 3 at 1:07 P.M., Colonel E. Porter Alexander, a young man in his late twenties, ordered his gunners to open fire. For the next 90 minutes, according to historian Steven Woodworth, 150 Confederate guns created "the heaviest artillery bombardment ever heard on the North American continent." The cannon produced so much smoke, that Rebel gunners were sometimes uncertain whether they were hitting their targets. In fact, as the cannon were fired repeatedly, their wheels dug into the ground, causing many shots to arc behind the Union line, where they exploded without doing much damage.

Then, at 2:30 P.M., the artillery barrage ended as suddenly as it had begun. A silence fell across the field, followed by Lee ordering Longstreet to assemble the division selected to advance toward the Union center. Their commander was 38-year-old George Pickett, a flamboyant Virginian who wore perfume and curled his hair. He had eagerly accepted the opportunity to lead the charge. Pickett's division stepped forward out of a line of trees into the open, his lines of men numbering near 14,000 strong.

At first they moved in a steady drum-beat march, then increased their pace to a double-quick, then began running straight for the Union center, where massed Federals were waiting behind a stone wall, reminiscent of the Rebels entrenched on Marye's Heights at Fredericksburg seven months earlier. The Confederates converged at a point along the wall where two sides angled, a site later called "The Angle." While some Southerners reached the wall, many were cut down on the field.

When the retreat was completed only 7,000 of Pickett's men had returned to the woods they had emerged from less than an hour earlier. Two out of every three of Pickett's men, three of his brigadier generals, and all 13 of his colonels were either killed or wounded. Those men who managed to stumble back to their lines were met by General Lee on his horse, riding back and forth in their path, according to historian James McPherson, telling his men, "It's all my fault. It is I who have lost this fight, and you must help me out of it the best way you can. All good men must rally." Lee and Longstreet prepared for a Union counterattack. When Lee told a dazed and confused Pickett to regroup his division, the Virginia commander's response was clear and to the point, as historian James McPherson notes: "General Lee, I have no division now."

Meade is Victorious

There was further fighting at Gettysburg on July 3, including a massive cavalry engagement between J.E.B. Stuart's horsemen and Michigan troops under the command of a young general named George Armstrong Custer. But Stuart also failed to rout the Federals. It was a Union victory.

But the victory at Gettysburg came at a high cost of manpower. Through three days of fighting, more than 51,000 casualties had been inflicted, including 23,000 on the

Victory on the Fourth of July

As news of the Union victory at Gettysburg spread across the North and South, word of another significant win for the Yankees soon followed on its heels.

Two months earlier General Ulysses S. Grant had captured Jackson, Mississippi, after an extensive campaign in the western theater of the war. This victory had opened the way for an attack on Vicksburg, a major port city on the Mississippi and one of the last significant Confederate strongholds on the river. On May 16, just two days after the fall of Jackson, Grant engaged a Rebel army of 20,000 under the command of General John C. Pemberton at Champion's Hill, just west of Vicksburg. Pemberton was forced to retreat to the city.

For the next six weeks Grant surrounded Vicksburg and laid a siege. Southerners in the city tried to hold out as best they could. Food became a major problem, with the citizens reduced eventually to eating horses, mules, dogs, cats, and rats. With Grant ordering regular mortar attacks into Vicksburg, the residents had to dig caves and tunnels into hillsides to serve as shelters. The Union men outside the city called Vicksburg "Prairie Dog Town."

With no Confederate Army able to counterattack Grant's significant force of 70,000 men, the people inside Vicksburg lost hope. Starving, Pemberton's men approached their commander about a surrender. Pemberton chose to give up the city on July 4, the day following the Gettysburg battle, thinking that the Yankees would give better terms on Independence Day. With the fall of Vicksburg, one of the last Confederate holdouts on the river, Port Hudson, surrendered on July 8. In Washington, President Lincoln was ecstatic, noting: "The Father of Waters again goes unvexed to the sea." General Winfield Scott's original strategy, the Anaconda Plan, had finally become reality.

Grant's campaign to capture Vicksburg is one of the most successful of the war. His army suffered fewer than 10,000 casualties, yet had killed or wounded an equal number of Confederates, and captured another 37,000 of the enemy.

Union side and 28,000 among the Rebels. Not only had the Southern army taken higher casualties by number and as a percentage of their total number of men, but these losses represented men killed, wounded, and missing who were becoming increasingly difficult to replace. From its opening salvos, the Civil War had always been a fight of attrition. The South had a limited number of men from which to draw its armies. And, by the summer of 1863, the gap between the number of troops the Confederacy needed to continue its fight against the Yankees and the number of men available was not only widening, it was reaching critical mass.

7

Grant and Lee's War

Following the surrender of Vicksburg on July 4, 1863, the future of the Confederacy looked dim. A Rebel private captured in the Mississippi city wrote, notes historian James McPherson: "I see no prospect now of the South ever sustaining itself. We have lost the Mississippi and our nation is Divided and they is not a nuf [enough] left to fight for." After the loss at Gettysburg, another Confederate soldier wrote to his sister: "We got a bad whipping... They are awhiping us... at every point... I hope they would make peace so that we that is alive yet would get home agane." In Richmond, President Davis struggled with despair.

"RIVER OF BLOOD"

As for President Lincoln, one constant he had come to rely on throughout more than two years of war was General Ulysses S. Grant. After Vicksburg's capture, as historian Harry Williams notes, Lincoln said enthusiastically: "Grant is my man and I am his the rest of the war." In October 1863 Lincoln put Grant in command of all Union forces located between the Appalachian Mountains and the Mississippi River.

Almost immediately following the Vicksburg victory Grant's forces were on their way to Chattanooga, situated on the border between Tennessee and Georgia. Chattanooga was an important rail center. In mid-August Union Major General William S. Rosecrans was also on the march with his Army of the Cumberland, headed toward the Rebel army he had encountered in the field at Murfreesboro eight months earlier. Despite the fact that Rosecrans's army numbered 75,000 and Confederate General Braxton Bragg's was only 40,000, the Union commander was slow to move against the Rebels. But he was able to dislodge Bragg from Chattanooga on September 9.

Clearly, Bragg needed reinforcements. President Davis immediately dispatched General Longstreet and more than 12,000 men by rail to join Bragg's army. Since Union forces controlled the rail line in eastern Tennessee and Cumberland Gap, the Confederates were forced to travel an additional 1,000 miles (1,600 km) from Virginia to Atlanta, then to Chattanooga, and some troops did not even complete the trip due to a lack of trains. But Bragg's force swelled to nearly 60,000 men.

Not long after the arrival of Longstreet's men the two armies clashed in a battle alongside a stream known as Chickamauga Creek. According to legend, the word *chickamauga* was Cherokee for "river of blood." By September 19 the fight was on, following an encounter between Major General George Thomas's forces and Confederate cavalry commanded by Major General Nathan Bedford Forrest.

The two-day fight was extremely bloody, producing some of the highest casualty rates of the war. The first day brought gains and losses on the field for both sides, but the battle was determined when Rosecrans moved men out of line to fill a gap that was actually no gap at all. General Longstreet noted the breach and ordered his men to fill it, causing the Union line to collapse. Only a spirited resistance by General Thomas's corps kept the Northern army from complete annihilation. For his efforts that day, Thomas gained a nickname: "The Rock of Chickamauga."

CHATTANOOGA

Union losses included more than 16,000 men killed, wounded, or missing. Confederate losses were higher, totaling more than 18,400, but Bragg and Longstreet had managed a singular and much needed victory. Following the battle Rosecrans rushed his army to shelter in Chattanooga, a move the Confederates used to their advantage. Rebel forces soon bottled up Rosecrans and his men in the city and laid a siege, just as Grant had done months earlier at Vicksburg. Confederates took the high ground around the city, including control of 1,100-foot (335-m) high Lookout Mountain and the 400-ft (120-m) high Missionary Ridge, which extended on for 6 miles (10 km).

Lincoln soon ordered a rescue mission to relieve Rosecrans' army. In the meantime the president removed Rosecrans from command, replacing him with the more reliable Thomas. Then he sent Grant, newly in command of the Military Division of the Mississippi, with troops to help the trapped Federals fight their way out of Chattanooga. Grant arrived on October 23, on crutches from a riding accident. Within a week he had ordered men to punch a hole in Confederate defenses, allowing a supply route to open up, which the Yankees called the "Cracker Line." Then Hooker arrived with units of the Army of the Potomac, as well as General William Tecumseh Sherman's Army of the Tennessee, Grant's old command.

By November 23, Union forces had massed in Chattanooga and the battle began, with Grant sending Hooker's men up Lookout Mountain and Sherman's and Thomas's men toward Missionary Ridge. The Federals managed to gain Lookout

The Gettysburg Address

With so many killed during the three-day Battle of Gettysburg, Congress determined to establish a national cemetery at the town, where the valiant Union dead could be buried. On November 19, 1863, at the cemetery's dedication, President Lincoln gave the speech that is now known as the Gettysburg Address:

Fourscore and seven years ago our fathers brought forth on this continent a new nation, conceived in liberty, and dedicated to the proposition that all men are created equal.

Now we are engaged in a great civil war, testing whether that nation, or any nation so conceived and so dedicated, can long endure. We are met on a great battlefield of that war. We have come to dedicate a portion of that field as a final resting place for those who here gave their lives that the nation might live. It is altogether fitting and proper that we should do this.

But, in a larger sense, we can not dedicate—we can not consecrate—we can not hallow—this ground. The brave men, living and dead, who struggled here, have consecrated it, far above our poor power to add or detract. The world will little note, nor long remember, what we say here, but it can never forget what they did here. It is for us the living, rather, to be dedicated here to the unfinished work which they who fought here have thus far so nobly advanced. It is rather for us to be here dedicated to the great task remaining before us—that from these honored dead we take increased devotion to that cause for which they gave the last full measure of devotion—that we here highly resolve that these dead shall not have died in vain—that this nation, under God, shall have a new birth of freedom—and that government of the people, by the people, for the people, shall not perish from the earth.

Mountain through a fight many referred to later as the "Battle Above the Clouds," as the heights were shrouded with fog. Thomas's forces pushed the Rebels off Missionary Ridge through a gallant direct frontal assault toward Confederate rifle pits. Rebel cannon at the top of the ridge were unable to train down at a low enough angle to blast the encroaching Yankees off the ridge.

Bragg lost the fight, in part because he had earlier sent Longstreet with his 15,000 men to drive another Union force (under Burnside's command) out of Knoxville, Tennessee. Longstreet had thought the move foolhardy, since it left Bragg with fewer men just as the Union forces were gaining in number. The battle resulted in the loss of 6,700 Confederates. While Bragg himself managed to escape, the Union victory ensured Northern control of eastern Tennessee.

GRANT LEADS THE ARMY

Grant was even more "Lincoln's man" following his superb victory at Chattanooga. The president had searched for a capable commander for three years—one who could meet the challenge of Robert E. Lee head-on—and had finally found his general in Grant. On March 9, 1864, Grant attended a ceremony at the White House during which he was promoted to the rank of lieutenant general, placing the successful westerner over all Federal troops. General William Tecumseh Sherman, an equally tenacious commander, took over Grant's duties as head of the Military Division of the Mississippi. Now Lincoln had two seasoned veterans he could rely on in command. Grant soon set about organizing a grand strategy.

Shortages Versus New Forces

The war had taken a dire direction for the South. The Confederacy was suffering from manpower shortages, as well as shortages in everything else, from food to munitions. The Union blockade of the Rebel coastline was in place, and the Mississippi had fallen under the control of the Union navy. Gettysburg, Vicksburg, Chattanooga, and other field battles had provided the North with important victories during the second half of 1863. Inflation was crippling the South, having risen an average of 58 percent during the three months following the loss at Gettysburg. By March 1864 a barrel of flour in Richmond, if one could even be found, sold for $250 (equivalent to about $4,250 today). Just four months earlier it had sold for less than a third of that amount.

In contrast, by the summer of 1863 the North had begun a new strategy, one designed to tap a valuable human resource—the enlistment of black soldiers. During the first two years of the war Lincoln had steered clear of accepting black troops into the Federal army, but, by early 1863, increasing pressures had convinced him of the value of arming black men. Lincoln informed his military governor of Tennessee in March, as noted by historian Roy Basler: "The colored population is the great available and yet unavailed of, force for restoring the Union. The bare sight of 50,000 armed and drilled black soldiers upon the banks of the Mississippi, would end the rebellion at once." During the last two years of the conflict approximately 190,000 blacks, both free and former slaves, served in the Union Army and navy. Their contribution is considered invaluable to the Northern war effort.

Northern Strategy

Grant's overall strategy was based on using the North's superior numbers to attack the Confederacy on multiple fronts and bring the South to its knees. The plan consisted of three parts. The Army of the James (River), consisting of 30,000 men, was to advance up the James River toward Richmond, a return to McClellan's earlier "Peninsula Campaign." Sherman, still in Chattanooga, was to march his Army of the Tennessee south into Georgia toward Atlanta, an important manufacturing and rail center. Meanwhile Meade's Army of the Potomac was to march toward Lee's forces, with Grant moving along with them. Grant told Meade, as noted by historian Tyler Dennett: "Lee's Army will be your objective point. Wherever Lee goes, there you will go also."

Grant sent additional, smaller armies into the field, as well, including General Nathanial Banks along Texas' Red River and General Franz Sigel, a German commander who was dispatched into the Shenandoah Valley to destroy the region's capacity to provide food for the Rebel army. Grant also ordered an end to all prisoner exchanges. He was determined to take advantage of the South's lack of manpower. Since the opening salvos of the conflict, the ultimate end of the Civil War had always hinged on attrition—that the South never had enough men to fully execute the war, especially if it became a long-term conflict. Now, for the first time during the war, a Union commander had organized a strategy based on establishing simultaneous, coordinated fronts, all designed to overstretch Confederate forces and bring about an end to the war.

Back to the Wilderness

On May 3 the strategies and the armies to carry them out were in place, from Texas to Georgia to Virginia. Grant crossed the Rapidan River that day and readied to march with Meade. Both Meade's army and Lee's forces were encamped in the vicinity of the Wilderness, where the battle of Chancellorsville had been fought nearly a year earlier. Here Grant's 120,000 men engaged Lee's 66,000 first on May 5. The fight became a confused melee of men and munitions. The woods were so thick that men could not see 50 ft (15 m) in any

Civil War Battles 1861–1865

This map shows the location of the major battles discussed in this book. There were some 10,500 armed conflicts in the Civil War. Of these, 384 were identified as major battles, and they took place across 26 states. Virginia (123 battles), Tennessee (38), Missouri (29) and Georgia (28) were the main areas of conflict, death, and destruction. Note that the North and South often used different names for the same battle, for example Shiloh (Pittsburg Landing) and Seven Pines (Fair Oaks).

direction. There were no interior lines, just masses of troops here and there and lots of smoke, especially after the woods caught on fire due to artillery explosions. Grant lost 17,000 men during the desperate fighting.

After battling tooth-and-nail with Lee for two days, Grant moved his forces by his left flank and skirted around Lee. He had no intention of breaking off the fight or giving Lee any time to recover. The two armies next converged at a strategic crossroads at Spotsylvania Court House. Here, Lee was almost overwhelmed. He was compelled to come to the front himself, announcing that he would lead a charge, but his men told him to remove himself from harm's way, only to take up the fight with renewed purpose, staving off the Union assault.

Yet the battle dragged on for two weeks with fighting on and off. The casualties mounted, with Grant's men suffering 17,500 killed or wounded out of an army of 110,000. No reliable Confederate casualty rate exists—this became more and more common during the last stage of the war. Once more Grant eventually moved by his left flank, forcing Lee again to move to keep his army between the Federals and Richmond.

Cold Harbor and Petersburg

On June 3 Grant ordered a direct frontal assault against an entrenched Lee at Cold Harbor, just west of the Confederate capital. (Just days earlier, General J.E.B. Stuart, Lee's great cavalry commander, had been killed at Yellow Tavern, a suburb of Richmond.) The night before the Federal advance at Cold Harbor some Yankee men pinned notes to the backs of their uniforms, providing their names and addresses in case they were killed. When the assault at Cold Harbor took place approximately 7,000 Northern troops fell in less than 10 minutes. In his *Memoirs*, published after the war, Grant

Southerners review the ruins of Richmond. After a long siege, Union forces captured the town in April 1865. Retreating Confederate forces were ordered to burn bridges and other key buildings. The fires went unchecked, causing serious damage.

only admitted one mistake as a commander—ordering the charge at Cold Harbor. But the victory there would be the last for Robert E. Lee. Nine days later Grant's forces met up with General Benjamin Butler's Army of the James.

On June 15 the Federals launched an assault toward the Virginia community of Petersburg, south of Richmond by 30 miles (48 km). Petersburg was an important rail junction that had helped protect the Confederate capital throughout the war. If the town could be captured by Grant, Richmond would be extremely vulnerable. But the assault was bungled, perhaps due to "Cold Harbor Syndrome," where earlier losses had been devastating. Rather than Petersburg falling easily to the Yankees, Grant was forced to order a siege. General Lee had no choice but to remain in Petersburg and its vicinity, since moving out of the region would leave Richmond vulnerable to attack. Through six weeks of almost constant fighting Grant had managed to checkmate Lee into inaction, through his tenacity and sheer numbers of men.

SHERMAN'S MARCH

Even as Grant and Lee had taken up the fight in early May, General Sherman had set out from Chattanooga, bound for Atlanta. He moved similarly to Grant, by his left flank, skirting repeatedly around a Confederate force led by General Joseph Johnston, who had commanded troops in Virginia before Robert E. Lee. At times Johnston himself fell back to avoid a fight against Sherman's superior numbers. There were engagements, as well, as at New Hope Church, 25 miles (40 km) northeast of Atlanta, where Johnston held Sherman back for two weeks. Then, on June 27, Sherman ordered a direct frontal assault toward Johnston's army entrenched on Kennesaw Mountain, where the Union commander misjudged Johnston to be overextended. Perhaps he thought he might accomplish an assault as successful as Missionary Ridge, but he was wrong. The Federals were routed. Sherman shrugged the fight off and moved forward, around Johnston's army, ever toward Atlanta.

On July 17 a frustrated President Davis replaced Johnston, convinced that his general was not fighting hard enough, with 33-year-old Texan Lieutenant General John Bell Hood. Hood had fought throughout the war, and had a reputation for tenacity. He had lost the use of his left arm during the Gettysburg battle and had his right leg amputated after Chickamauga. Hood would fight even when dramatically outnumbered, but such fights only caused Hood's army to dwindle in number as Sherman came closer to Atlanta. Prior to the war Atlanta had been home to 12,000 citizens, but many had evacuated the city with Sherman's men headed their way. By September 2, Union forces had captured the Georgia city, and Sherman sent a telegram to the War Department in Washington, notes historian Geoffrey Ward: "Atlanta is ours, and fairly won."

Sherman's success at Atlanta could not have been better timed for Abraham Lincoln. The President was running for reelection, even in the midst of civil war. Although the direction of the three-and-a-half year conflict was turning in favor of the North, there were still Northern critics who advocated ending the conflict immediately and allowing the South to remain separate from the Union. Complicating matters even more was Lincoln's opponent. The Democratic nominee was none other than George McClellan.

As Sherman launched his campaign he cut off his own supply line, intending for his men to live off the land. Marching across Georgia, Sherman's army stretched 60 miles (100 km) wide. His men stripped the region of everything that might be used to support the Confederate war effort, such as railroad lines, telegraph poles, factories, and other means of production, along with food and livestock taken from farms and plantations to feed them. For weeks Sherman's "March to the Sea" left a trail of devastation, fulfilling the Union commander's intention, notes historian Geoffrey Ward, to "make Georgia howl."

Welcome Support

In the meantime, Lincoln had won reelection. Despite his fears that he would not be reelected, the president managed to defeat McClellan with a wide majority of electoral votes—212 to 21. The former Union commander only carried three states—Delaware, Kentucky, and New Jersey. While Lincoln had won with only 41 percent of the popular vote in 1860, he pulled 55 percent in 1864. Perhaps most telling was the soldier vote. Ballots had been prepared for Federal soldiers, who had to choose between their commander-in-chief and their former military commander. Overwhelmingly, the soldiers supported Lincoln, who won 78 percent of their ballots. Even among the troops of the Army of the Potomac, McClellan's old command, only 29 percent voted for McClellan. The election made it clear to Lincoln that Northerners supported a successful conclusion to the war and had rejected any suggestion that the South be allowed to go its own way.

By December 21 Sherman's men were outside Savannah. After the local Rebel army of 15,000 abandoned the city, Sherman sent Lincoln a telegram bearing welcome news, notes James McPherson: "I beg to present you as a Christmas gift the city of Savannah." The Union Army then turned north into the Carolinas, where they occupied Columbia, the state capital, on February 17. Less than a week later Union troops arrived from Nashville, Tennessee, by train and captured Wilmington, the only major North Carolina port not under Union control. Slowly, the noose was tightening around the Confederacy.

THE END OF THE CONFLICT

The year 1865 would deliver the war's conclusion. In January Congress passed the Thirteenth Amendment, which called for the end of slavery. The amendment would be ratified by the states by year's end. By spring 1865 as many as two out of every five Rebel soldiers had packed up and left the war for home. Desperately short on manpower, the Confederate Congress passed a bill allowing blacks to enlist in the Southern Army, but the decision was made too late to make a difference. The Confederacy came crashing down within weeks of the political move. These were the final days of the prolonged siege between Lee and Grant.

In late March Lee made the decision to abandon Petersburg and Richmond and break out to the west, hoping to meet up with the remnants of Joe Johnston's army and fight another day. When Confederates attacked Fort Stedman along the Union siege lines, Grant knew the time had come to end the siege. With Lee moving, Union forces engaged

A Disease-Ridden War

It is one of the cold facts of the Civil War that almost twice as many men died from disease than from wounds inflicted on the battlefield. The poor state of medical facilities and personnel help explain why. There were no army hospitals before the war began, and military doctors were few.

In April 1861, the U.S. Army had only 113 surgeons, and two dozen of them went with the Confederacy. By 1865, the two armies were served by 15,000 surgeons. Still, the state of Civil War-era medicine was appalling. There was little understanding of germs, and doctors routinely moved from patient to patient without washing their hands, which helped to spread infections. Actual medicines were few and many were ineffective against such widespread diseases as tuberculosis, typhoid, and smallpox.

him at Five Forks, west of Petersburg, where defense lines laid down by General Pickett failed to hold on April 1.

Grant responded by ordering an assault along all points on April 2. Lee and his ragtag army fled across the Appomattox River, even as President Davis and his cabinet abandoned Richmond. Confederates burned the city as they departed on April 3, before the arrival of Federal troops, leaving behind the smoking remains of the Rebel dream. Three days later Lee was caught by Union forces at Sayler's Creek, where he lost 8,000 men, approximately one-third of his remaining forces. With no options left, and with his army virtually cut off at every turn, Lee sent a note to Grant asking to meet with the Union commander. The two leaders met on April 9 in the front parlor of Appomattox Court House, a sleepy crossroads in Virginia, and, with the stroke of a pen, Lee signed a surrender document under Grant's terms.

"A New Birth of Freedom"

For four straight years, the people of the United States had fought against one another in a civil war that left 620,000 men dead. More Americans died during this bloody nineteenth century conflict than in all other American wars combined. They fought on battlefields across the South and on Northern soil, in Maryland, Pennsylvania, Missouri, and Kentucky. Those battles revealed the honorable manhood of the armies that clashed across bloodied ground. The blue- or gray-clad soldiers who fought, as well as those who supported them, did so for reasons that were often personal and individualistic. Yet for many, both Northerners and Southerners, the war was about America's future—whether or not the United States would continue to be divided "half slave and half free." In the end, the Civil War decided the arguments over slavery, even as, in the words of President Abraham Lincoln, it established "a new birth of freedom."

Chronology

1820 The Missouri Compromise is negotiated, allowing Maine to be admitted to the Union as a free state and Missouri as a slave state in 1821

1831

January Social reformer William Lloyd Garrison publishes the first issue of the abolitionist newspaper, *The Liberator*

TIMELINE

1820
The Missouri Compromise is negotiated, allowing Maine to be admitted to the Union as a free state and Missouri as a slave state in 1821

January 1831
William Lloyd Garrison publishes the first issue of the abolitionist newspaper, *The Liberator*

1838
The Underground Railroad expands

1852
Harriet Beecher Stowe publishes *Uncle Tom's Cabin*

1857
The Supreme Court rules in *Dred Scott v. Sandford* that blacks are not U.S. citizens, and slaveholders have the right to take existing slaves into free areas of the county

October 1859
John Brown seizes arsenal at Harpers Ferry, Virginia. Robert E. Lee, then a Federal Army regular leads the troops and captures Brown

1820 1830 1840 1850 1859

1836 The House passes a gag rule that automatically tables or postpones action on all petitions relating to slavery without hearing them

1838 The Underground Railroad expands including routes to Mexico and overseas

1850 Congress implements several measures forming the Compromise of 1850

1852 Harriet Beecher Stowe publishes antislavery novel *Uncle Tom's Cabin*

1854 The Kansas–Nebraska Act passes Congress and thus overturns the Missouri Compromise, opening the Northern territory to slavery

November 1860
Abraham Lincoln is elected president

March 1861
Lincoln inaugurated as sixteenth president of the United States, and delivers his First Inaugural Address

April 12, 1861
South Carolina's Fort Sumter is fired upon by the Confederates. The Civil War begins

April 6–7, 1862
Ulysses Grant defeats Confederates in Battle of Pittsburgh Landing (Shiloh)

September 17, 1862
The bloodiest day in U.S. military history as Gen. Robert E. Lee and the Confederate Armies are stopped at Antietam in Maryland by McClellan

July 1–3, 1863
Confederates are defeated at the Battle of Gettysburg in Pennsylvania

March 9, 1864
President Lincoln appoints Grant to command all of the armies of the United States

January 31, 1865
Thirteenth Amendment to the United States Constitution, to abolish slavery

April 14, 1865
John Wilkes Booth shoots President Lincoln at Ford's Theater

1860 1861 1862 1863 1864 1865

1855 As Kansas prepares for elections, Border Ruffians from Missouri enter the territory so as to influence the election. This begins the Bloody Kansas period

1856

May South Carolina Representative Preston Brooks attacks Massachusetts Senator Charles Sumner on the Senate floor and beats him with a cane

1857 The Supreme Court rules in *Dred Scott v. Sandford* that blacks are not U.S. citizens, and slaveholders have the right to take existing slaves into free areas of the county

1859

October John Brown seizes arsenal at Harpers Ferry, Virginia. Robert E. Lee, then a Federal Army regular leads the troops and captures Brown

1860

November Abraham Lincoln is elected president

December South Carolina passes ordinance of secession by which the state leaves the Union

1861

January Florida, Alabama, Georgia, and Louisiana secede from the Union

February Texas votes to secede from the Union. The Confederate States of America is formed with Jefferson Davis as president

March Lincoln inaugurated as sixteenth president of the United States, and delivers his First Inaugural Address

April 12 At 4:30 A.M., South Carolina's Fort Sumter is fired upon by the Confederates. The Civil War begins. Virginia secedes from the Union five days later

May Arkansas and North Carolina secede from the Union

June Tennessee secedes from the Union

July 21 The Union suffers a defeat at Bull Run (Manassas)

August Confederates win battle of Wilson's Creek

1862

February 6 Victory for General Ulysses S. Grant in Tennessee, capturing Fort Henry and, 10 days later, Fort Donelson

March 9 The Confederate ironclad *Merrimac* (formerly the *Virginia*) battles the Union ironclad *Monitor* to a draw. The Peninsular Campaign begins

April 6–7 Grant defeats Confederates in Battle of Pittsburgh Landing (Shiloh)

April 24 Flag Officer David Farragut moves vessels up the Mississippi River then takes New Orleans

May 31 The Battle of Seven Pines (Fair Oaks)

June 1 Lee assumes command of the Army of Northern Virginia

June 25–July 1 The Seven Days Battles

August 29–30 Union forces are defeated at the Second Battle of Bull Run in northern Virginia

September 17 The bloodiest day in U.S. military history as Lee and the Confederate Armies are stopped at Antietam in Maryland by McClellan

September 22 Emancipation Proclamation freeing slaves is issued by President Lincoln

December 13 The Army of the Potomac under command of General Burnside suffers a costly defeat at Fredericksburg

1863

January 1 President Lincoln issues the final Emancipation Proclamation

January 29 Grant is placed in command of the Army of the West, with orders to capture Vicksburg

May 1–4 The Union Army under General Hooker is decisively defeated by Lee's much smaller forces at the Battle of Chancellorsville

May 10 The South suffers a huge blow as Stonewall Jackson dies from wounds he received during the battle of Chancellorsville

June 3 With 75,000 Confederates Lee launches his second invasion of the North, heading into Pennsylvania

July 1–3 The tide of war turns against the South as the Confederates are defeated at the Battle of Gettysburg in Pennsylvania

July 4 Vicksburg, the last Confederate stronghold on the Mississippi River, surrenders to Grant after a six-week siege

September 19–20 A decisive Confederate victory at Chickamauga, Tennessee

November 23–25 The battle of Chattanooga

1864

March 9 President Lincoln appoints Grant to command all of the armies of the United States

May 4 Grant opens a massive, coordinated campaign in Virginia directly against Lee

May 5–6 The Battle of the Wilderness

May 8–12 The Battle of Spotsylvania

June 1–3 The Battle of Cold Harbor

June 15 Union forces miss an opportunity to capture Petersburg, resulting in a nine-month Union siege of the city

September 2 Atlanta is captured by Sherman's Army

November 8 Lincoln is re-elected president, defeating Democrat George B. McClellan

November 15 Sherman begins his March to the Sea

December 15–16 Confederate General John Bell Hood is defeated at Nashville by General George H. Thomas

December 21 Sherman reaches Savannah in Georgia, leaving a path of destruction 300 miles (480 km) long and 60 miles (100 km) wide all the way from Atlanta

1865

January 31 The U.S. Congress approves the Thirteenth Amendment to the United States Constitution, to abolish slavery

March 25 The last offensive for Lee's Army of Northern Virginia begins with an attack on the center of Grant's forces at Petersburg. Four hours later the attack is broken

April 2 Grant's forces begin a general advance and break through Lee's lines at Petersburg. Lee evacuates Petersburg. Richmond is evacuated

April 9 Lee surrenders his Confederate Army to Grant at the village of Appomattox Court House in Virginia

April 14 John Wilkes Booth shoots President Lincoln at Ford's Theatre

April 15 President Abraham Lincoln dies. Vice President Andrew Johnson assumes the presidency

Glossary

abolitionism The campaign to free slaves immediately.

Anaconda Plan A Northern strategy, developed at the start of the war, which involved a Union naval blockade of the entire Confederate coastline and control of the Mississippi River, to cut off Louisiana, Arkansas, and Texas from the remainder of the Confederacy.

artillery Large mounted guns or cannon; the part of an army that uses and manages such guns.

Bleeding Kansas Violence between proslavery and antislavery advocates in Kansas during the 1850s.

border state One of the four slave states—Missouri, Kentucky, Maryland, and Delaware—that did not secede from the Union.

casualty In military terms, any human loss on a battlefield, including those killed, wounded, missing, or captured.

Confederates or Confederacy Those who supported secession from the United States and who fought for the South during the Civil War.

Democrat Party A political party formed during the age of Andrew Jackson, which supported the Jackson presidency.

desert In military terms, to leave the ranks of an army without permission.

division A military unit, made up of several brigades or regiments plus supporting troops, and usually commanded by a major general.

emancipation The act of freeing individuals from service or slavery.

Emancipation Proclamation Official announcement made by President Abraham Lincoln in the fall of 1862 that "freed" all slaves held in states in rebellion against the United States.

Federals Troops who fought for the North or the Union side during the Civil War.

federal government Refers to the national government that holds power by the will of the people. State power is subordinate to federal power. During the Civil War the Federal Government was the government of the Union states only.

flank Either end of a line of massed soldiers, signified as an army's "left" or "right."

Free-Soilers A political party created during the 1840s and later replaced by the Republican Party. The Free-Soilers did not support the western expansion of slavery.

guerrilla A fighter who is not part of an organized or official military structure and often carries out acts of sabotage.

inauguration Ceremony that includes the swearing-in of a president at the opening of a new four-year term in office.

insubordination Resistance or disobedience to an authority; refusal to obey; disobedient or unruly behavior showing a lack of respect.

Kansas–Nebraska Act An 1854 act of Congress that created the territories of Kansas and Nebraska.

militia Troops provided on a state level.

Minie ball A cone-shaped projectile fired from a musket or rifle. It was invented by the French army captain, Claude Minie.

mortar A heavy, short cannon designed to lob large shells in a high arc over a short distance against enemy fortifications. It was often used during sieges.

musket A handheld weapon with a long, smoothbore barrel, which fires a lead projectile or bullet.

muzzle The end of a musket or rifle barrel from which the bullet is fired.

"On to Richmond" strategy A recurring Union strategy, involving a direct advance from the North to capture Richmond, the Confederate capital. The purpose was to force an end to the war.

picket A forward position on a battlefield meant to serve as a watch on an enemy's advance.

plantation A large estate, often found in the U.S. South during the eighteenth and early nineteenth centuries, where slavery was typically in practice.

pontoon boats Flat-bottomed boats used to create a floating bridge across a river for soldiers, artillery, horses, and wagons to cross.

Popular sovereignty A political theory that encouraged the residents of a western territory to vote on whether or not they wanted slavery to exist in their future state.

rebels A common term for Southerners who supported the Confederacy during the Civil War.

reconnaissance Gathering intelligence about an enemy, its strength, and its position.

regiment A unit of an army, made up of several battalions or squadrons of soldiers organized into one large group, and usually commanded by a colonel. A regiment is smaller than a brigade.

Republicans Members of the Republican Party, which was formed during the early 1850s and was generally a Northern party in its base.

rifle A handheld weapon with a long barrel, which fires a lead projectile or bullet. A rifle's barrel is cut inside with spiral grooves, or rifling, which provides the bullet with greater accuracy and speed.

rifle pits Shallow trenches manned by riflemen.

secede To separate or remove a state from a larger state.

sharpshooter An expert rifleman capable of firing accurately at targets at great distances.

Shenandoah Valley A fertile valley in western Virginia, lying west of the Blue Ridge Mountains.

shore batteries Groupings of cannon or artillery, situated along a coast.

siege A military operation in which an army surrounds a town or other fortified place to cut off access and force a surrender.

skirmish A small-scale military engagement with less scope or action than a full-fledged battle.

Special Order No. 191 A set of orders issued by Robert E. Lee in the spring of 1862, which called for his forces to be divided and dispatched in several directions.

subordinate An enlisted man serving under an officer of higher rank.

sunken road A rural road or lane, which has formed a depression in the ground through prolonged use.

Thirteenth Amendment An amendment to the U.S. Constitution of January 1865 that brought an official end to slavery in the United States.

Union Common name in the 1800s for the United States.

Valley Campaign A Confederate campaign in the Shenandoah Valley during the spring of 1862, led by General Stonewall Jackson.

Whig Party American political party, created during the 1830s to oppose President Andrew Jackson's political views. The party remained in existence for about 20 years. The Republican Party, established in the early 1850s, included former Whigs.

Yankee A common term used by Southerners to refer to Northerners.

Bibliography

Altman, Linda Jacobs. *Slavery and Abolition in American History.* Berkeley Heights, NJ: Enslow Publishers, 1999.

Basler, Roy P. *Collected Works of Abraham Lincoln.* New Brunswick, NJ: Rutgers University Press, 1955.

Bearss, Edwin C. *Fields of Honor: Pivotal Battles of the Civil War.* Washington, D.C.: National Geographic Society, 2006.

Calhoun, John C. (H. Lee Cheek, Ed.) *Calhoun: Selected Writings and Speeches.* Washington, D.C.: Regnery Publishing, Inc., 2003.

Dabney, Robert L. *Life and Campaigns of Lieut.-Gen. Thomas J. Jackson.* New York: Blalock & Co., 1866.

Davis, David Brion, ed. *The Boisterous Sea of Liberty: A Documentary History of America from Discovery Through the Civil War.* New York: Oxford University Press, 2000.

Dennett, Tyler, ed. *Lincoln and the Civil War in the Diaries and Letters of John Hay.* New York: Da Capo Press, 1988.

Earle, Peter. *Robert E. Lee.* New York: Saturday Review Press, 1973.

Foote, Shelby. *The Civil War, A Narrative, Volume II: Fredericksburg to Meridian.* New York: Random House, 1963.

Freeman, Douglas Southall. *R.E. Lee: A Biography.* New York: Charles Scribner's Sons, 1934–35.

Goodwin, Doris Kearns. *Team of Rivals: The Political Genius of Abraham Lincoln.* New York: Simon & Schuster, 2005.

Hine, Darlene Clark. *The African-American Odyssey.* Upper Saddle River, NJ: Prentice Hall, 2005.

Hoehling, A. A., ed. *Last Train from Atlanta.* New York: Stackpole Books, 1992. Reprint of 1958 edition.

Longstreet, James. *The Battle of Fredericksburg.* In Robert Underwood Johnson and Clarence Clough Buel, *Battles and Leaders of the Civil War, Volume III.* Whitefish, MT: Kessinger Publishing Company, 2004.

McPherson, James. *Ordeal by Fire: The Civil War and Reconstruction.* New York: McGraw-Hill, 1992.

Murfin, James F. *The Gleam of Bayonets: The Battle of Antietam and Robert E. Lee's Maryland Campaign, September 1862.* New York: Thomas Yoseloff Publishers, 1965.

Remini, Robert. *A Short History of the United States.* New York: HarperCollins, 2008.

Rice, Earle. *Robert E. Lee: First Soldier of the Confederacy.* Greensboro, NC: Morgan Reynolds, 2005.

Roland, Charles P. *Reflections on Lee: An Assessment.* Mechanicsburg, PA: Stackpole Books, 1993.

Thomas, Benjamin. *Abraham Lincoln: A Biography.* New York: Alfred A. Knopf, Inc., 1952.

Thomas, Emory M. *Robert E. Lee, A Biography.* New York: W. W. Norton & Company, 1995.

Walker, John G. *Jackson's Capture of Harper's Ferry.* In Robert Underwood Johnson and Clarence Clough Buel, *Battles and Leaders of the Civil War, Volume II.* Whitefish, MT: Kessinger Publishing Company, 2004.

Ward, Geoffrey. *The Civil War.* New York: Random House Publishers, 1990.

Weinstein, Allen. *The Story of America: Freedom and Crisis From Settlement to Superpower.* New York: DK Publishing, Inc., 2002.

Williams, Harry. *Lincoln and His Generals.* New York: Random House Publishers, 1952.

Woodworth, Steve and Kenneth J. Winkle. *Atlas of the Civil War.* New York: Oxford University Press, 2004.

Further Resources

Anderson, Paul Christopher. *Robert E. Lee: Legendary Commander of the Confederacy.* Rosen Publishing Group, Inc., 2001.

Arnold, James R. *On to Richmond: The Civil War in the East, 1861–62.* Minneapolis: Lerner Publishing Group, 2001.

Clark, Philip. *American Civil War: Wars That Changed the World.* Darby, PA: Diane Publishing Company, 1998.

Doak, Robin Santos. *Thomas Stonewall Jackson: Confederate General.* Mankato, MN: Coughlan Publishing, 2005.

Dolan, Edward F. *American Civil War: A House Divided.* Minneapolis: Lerner Publishing Group, 1997.

Faust, Drew Gilpin. *This Republic of Suffering: Death and the American Civil War.* San Diego: Gale Group, 2008.

Ford, Carin T. *American Civil War: An Overview.* Berkeley Heights, NJ: Enslow Publishers, Inc., 2004.

Grabowski, Patricia A. *Robert E. Lee: Confederate General.* Broomall, PA: Chelsea House Publishers, 2000.

Gregson, Susan R. *Ulysses S. Grant.* Mankato, MN: Coughlan Publishing, 2000.

Hale, Sarah Elder. *Gettysburg: Bold Battle in the North.* Peterborough, NH: Cobblestone, 2005.

------ *Jefferson Davis and the Confederacy.* Peterborough, NH: Cobblestone, 2005.

Kantor, MacKinlay. *Lee and Grant at Appomattox.* New York: Sterling Publishing, 2007.

Kennedy, Robert, Jr. *American Heroes: Joshua Chamberlain and the American Civil War.* New York: Hyperion Books for Children, 2007.

McLeese, Don. *Ulysses S. Grant.* Shippensburg, PA: Rourke Publishing, LLC., 2005.

McPherson, James. *Fields of Fury: The American Civil War.* New York: Simon & Schuster Children's Publishing, 2002.

Ransom, Candice F. *Robert E. Lee.* Minneapolis: Lerner Publishing Group, 2006.

Ruffin, Frances. *Abraham Lincoln: From Pioneer to President.* New York: Sterling Publishing, 2007.

Stone, Tanya Lee. *Abraham Lincoln.* New York: DK Publishing, 2004.

Web sites

Abraham Lincoln:
http://www.abraham-lincoln.org/
http://www.abrahamlincolnsclassroom.org/

American Civil War:
http://www.americancivilwar.com/civil.html
http://www.civil-war.net/
http://www.civilwar.com/
http://www.civilwarhome.com

American Civil War Museum—Gettysburg
http://gettysburgmuseum.com/museum.asp

Battle of Gettysburg:
http://www.brotherswar.com/

Civil War Battles:
http://homepages.dsu.edu/jankej/civilwar/battles.htm

Timeline of the Civil War:
http://memory.loc.gov/ammem/cwphtml/tl1861.html

Ulysses S. Grant:
http://www.granthomepage.com/grantnews.htm

Picture Credits

Page

10: The Granger Collection, NYC/TopFoto
19: © CORBIS Inc.
23: The Granger Collection, NYC/TopFoto
34: Getty Images
36: The Granger Collection, NYC/TopFoto
43: Illustration by John James
55: The Granger Collection, NYC/TopFoto
60: The Granger Collection, NYC/TopFoto
68: The Granger Collection, NYC/TopFoto
73: The Granger Collection, NYC/TopFoto
77: The Granger Collection, NYC/TopFoto
82: The Granger Collection, NYC/TopFoto
89: The Granger Collection, NYC/TopFoto
90: The Granger Collection, NYC/TopFoto
96: The Granger Collection, NYC/TopFoto
100: Illustration by James Field
106: The Granger Collection, NYC/TopFoto
120: The Granger Collection, NYC/TopFoto
128: Courtesy of Abbott Studio, www.abbottsudio.com

Index

About the Author

Tim McNeese is associate professor of history at York College in York, Nebraska. Professor McNeese holds degrees from York College, Harding University, and Missouri State University. He has published more than 100 books and educational materials. His writing has earned him a citation in the library reference work, *Contemporary Authors* and multiple citations in *Best Books for Young Teen Readers*. In 2006, Tim appeared on the History Channel program, *Risk Takers, History Makers: John Wesley Powell and the Grand Canyon*. He was been a faculty member at the Tony Hillerman Writers Conference in Albuquerque. His wife, Beverly, is assistant professor of English at York College. They have two married children, Noah and Summer, and three grandchildren—Ethan, Adrianna, and Finn William. Tim and Bev have sponsored college study trips on the Lewis and Clark Trail and to the American Southwest. You may contact Professor McNeese at tdmcneese@york.edu.

About the Consultant

Richard Jensen is Research Professor at Montana State University, Billings. He has published 11 books on a wide range of topics in American political, social, military, and economic history, as well as computer methods. After taking a Ph.D. at Yale in 1966, he taught at numerous universities, including Washington, Michigan, Harvard, Illinois-Chicago, West Point, and Moscow State University in Russia.